Bloody Pommies!

Dorothy Dewing

Best wishes,
Dorothy Dewing

authorHOUSE®

AuthorHouse™ UK Ltd.
500 Avebury Boulevard
Central Milton Keynes, MK9 2BE
www.authorhouse.co.uk
Phone: 08001974150

©2009 Dorothy Dewing. All rights reserved.

No part of this book may be reproduced, stored in a retrieval system, or transmitted by any means without the written permission of the author.

First published by AuthorHouse 5/19/2009

ISBN: 978-1-4389-7694-5 (sc)

This book is printed on acid-free paper.

The true, honest, no-holds-barred, account of the experiences of a ten year old and her Mother aged 51, who emigrated to Australia in 1951 under the £10 assisted passage scheme, and how they dealt with the resentment and discrimination that they encountered during four years in a small New South Wales town.

The Author

Photo courtesy of Photo Magic

The author is married with 3 children and five grand-daughters, and on returning from Australia and completing her education, she started work at 16 with Phillips and Drew, a firm of stockbrokers in London. She was the first ever female to deal directly with the Dealers on the floor of the Stock Exchange, which was an all-male establishment up to that time, in the late 1950s.

She married a policeman in London, and they moved to Suffolk in 1960. After various part-time jobs whilst the family was growing up, she started working with Shell UK Exploration and Production at Lowestoft and on retirement was Head of Personnel Services, with full Chartered Membership of the Chartered Institute of Personnel and Development.

The Author was also a Justice of the Peace in Norfolk until she settled with her husband in Tenerife, where she now spends most of her time.

Bloody Pommies!

The term **"pommy"** has long been used by Australians to describe British people. They may, however, be making a slight mistake. The word is believed to be derived from the initials of the words **"Prisoner Of Mother England"** … which would suggest that it is maybe the Australians and their ancestors who more correctly deserve the title! When I was in Australia in the 1950s, it was used as a derogatory term, and usually accompanied by the word "bloody" or followed by the word "bastard", but nowadays most Brits regard it as an affectionate nickname, a joke, and rarely take offence.

Dorothy Dewing

*For Lyn, Wen and Pil –
No other Mother has ever been blessed with greater
treasures, nor been more proud of them.*

Acknowledgements

My sincere and lasting thanks go to:

My husband Rodney for his love, encouragement, help and support for me when all my time seemed to be devoted to the book and not to him;

My daughter Wendy, whose expertise in guiding me through the technical, grammatical and presentation minefields was essential and faultless – her wise words prevented me from 'coming unglued' countless times through all stages of the production of the book!;

My daughter Lynda, whose encouragement, advice and support for the project never left me, and ensured its completion;

My son Paul, for his encouragement and for the inspiration and expertise that went into designing the cover, and processing the photographs for printing;

My very good friend Jeanie in Australia, who untiringly researched facts that I could not properly remember or access – without her the book would lack the detail that is so important to create a feeling for the period in which the book is set. In addition, Jeanie devoted a considerable amount of time to reading the book and offering me her valued opinion on the appeal of the book to Australians;

My very good friends Carol and Mary in England, for having the patience to read every word, and to offer advice and comments on the book;

And finally, all those patient family members and friends who sat for hours listening to me going on and on about the book whilst it was being written!

Foreword

When Dorothy asked me to read and edit her book I felt honoured and delighted. Although I was not quite six years old when she and her mother stayed with us prior to returning to England, the Baker name was often spoken about in our household in the years which followed. Mrs Baker kept in touch and I still have Dorothy's school case, which has her name and Corowa address written inside.

This book will appeal to a wide range of readers of all ages and from varied backgrounds, as it is written in a style which is very easy to read and which vividly portrays the events as they occur, taking the reader from the author's birth and childhood in war-torn England, through her mother's decision for them to migrate to Australia to join Dorothy's brother Peter; the excitement of the voyage; the trials and tribulations of a mother having to find accommodation and work and a daughter having to enrol in a new school; the reunion with Dorothy's sister Joanie and her husband Fred, who followed them to Australia; their many experiences and the final decision to return to England.

I think that I was particularly interested in their experiences as both my father and my husband migrated from England. I can certainly draw comparisons with the discrimination faced by the Bakers and by my husband, who, like Peter, came out with the Big Brother Movement. Although I cannot verify all the incidents, I have lived in Corowa all my life, and so have been able to assist with accuracy as much as possible.

Thank you, Dorothy, for your friendship and for allowing me to share in this venture to record a slice of your interesting life.

Jeanie Binns

Contents

The Author..3
Bloody Pommies! 5
Acknowledgements..9
Foreword..11
Preface...15

Part 1: England (The Early Years)

Chapter One – Kent 19
Chapter 2 – London 24
Chapter 3 – The Parting 37
Chapter 4 – Postcards Galore! 41
Chapter 5 – Peter in Australia.................................45

Part Two: The Journey

Chapter 6 – Much Excitement! 53
Chapter 7 – Port Said 58
Chapter 8 – Aden and Ceylon.................................62
Chapter 9 – 'Water, water everywhere,
 and not a drop to drink' 66
Chapter 10 – Fremantle, Adelaide and Melbourne 71

Photos

Part Three: Australia

Chapter 11– The Sheep Farm..................................99
Chapter 12 – School 107
Chapter 13 – Abandoned 120

Chapter 14 – Settling In.................................125
Chapter 15 – More Babysitting......................140
Chapter 16 – Letters!....................................148
Chapter 17– Joyful Reunions 156
Chapter 18 – From bad to worse –
　　　　　　 and back again!....................169
Chapter 19 – On the move again 177
Chapter 20 – A New Arrival!.........................190
Chapter 21 – On the move yet again!.............199
Chapter 22 – Another Sad Parting 211
Chapter 23 – Hard Work 217
Chapter 24 – On our own again....................228

Part 4: The Journey Home

Chapter 25 – We are on our way back!..........241
Chapter 26 – Trouble Brewing 247

Part Five: Postscript

Mum..257
Peter...259
Joanie And Fred 264
Brenda..266
Aunty Cora 268
Me 270

Preface

They say that everybody has one book in them … well, this is mine. I have wanted to write it for many years, but now that I am living in tranquil, warm Tenerife I have the time and the enthusiasm for such a project. Time may have dimmed my memories, but some of them are indelibly fixed forever.

Despite the setbacks and challenges, there are many amusing moments so please persevere to the final chapters – it does have a happy ending!

Where I can remember names I have included them unless to do so would cause embarrassment.

Part 1

England (The Early Years)

Chapter One – Kent

The air raid siren wailed mournfully in the cold morning air. It was 10.30am on 6th March, 1941, in Rainham, Kent. My Mother, then aged 41, was in the last stages of labour, awaiting my birth, so she was unable to get to the air raid shelter in the garden. A bomb fell into the garden across the road, exploded, and shook Mum out of the bed … "*That explains a lot*," friends would say in later life!

I was born at 3.20pm that day, and my Mum, ever the proud and concerned lady, refused to allow herself to make any noise whatsoever at the end of her labour … in case it frightened the young children passing the bungalow on their way home from school. I was, as she told me often, a 'mistake', the result of my Dad coming home drunk one night and forcing his attentions on her. I was also the cause of her being discharged from her job in the Pay Office of the WRNS at Chatham Barracks, a fact she also reminded me of frequently in later years.

The bungalow was moderately sized, with an orchard behind it. There were 72 fruit trees, and it was a wonderful adventure playground for a young child to grow up in. There was an Anderson air-raid shelter in the garden, dug into the earth, and I have memories of being carried in the middle of the night, wrapped in a blanket, into the shelter when there were air-raids. I remember the damp, musty smell of the blankets, the black beetles that infested the place, and the welcome sound of the 'All Clear' siren when we could return into the bungalow again. I was to spend the first six years of my life in this bungalow, a happy child with a brother Peter who was nearly eight years older than me, and a sister Joanie who was ten years older than me, for company. I adored them both, and I lost my best friend and my hero when they both died in their sixties in 1994 within a month of each other.

Mum was the only child of Walter and Maud Kidd. Walter was a direct descendant of Captain Kidd, the notorious 17th century pirate. During the 1930s, some buried treasure had been discovered on an island and it was believed to be Captain Kidd's. An advertisement in the newspaper stated that if anyone could prove that they were directly descended from Captain Kidd they might receive a share of the treasure, so my Grandfather traced his ancestry directly back to Captain Kidd ... only to be told eventually that the treasure wasn't Captain Kidd's after all. Never mind ... the family now knew that they had a romantic background, and it gave another opportunity to my friends to say later on in my life ... *"That explains a lot!"*

I never knew any of my grandparents; they all died before I was born, so I never experienced that very special relationship that children often have with their grandparents. Walter John Kidd was the Managing

Director of Horlicks Malted Milk in Manchester, and Mum grew up in a privileged household, with Nannies and servants to take care of her. She never learned any of the domestic skills – she never needed them as a young woman growing up with other people taking care of all things menial – so she was neither a good cook, nor a good housekeeper. When she left school, she went to Pitman's College to learn secretarial skills, and then became her Father's Personal Assistant at Horlicks. When her Father retired, she continued to work at secretarial jobs. My Grandmother was a stern, unloving Mother, and when my Grandfather died two years after retiring, Grandmother became an alcoholic, and in effect, drank the family fortune away, so Mum inherited none of the wealth that she had taken for granted whilst growing up. Mum 'took the pledge' at the age of 21, promising never to touch alcohol, so disgusted was she with her Mother's drinking.

My paternal Grandfather, Peter Baker, was an Estate Manager in Derbyshire, and he, his wife and 9 children lived in a tied cottage on the estate. One day when Grandfather was out in a pony and trap on Estate duties, the pony reared up, throwing Grandfather out of the trap backwards, and this fall broke his neck, killing him. My Grandmother then had to vacate the tied cottage, and most of the older boys emigrated to Toronto in Canada. Two of the girls, my Auntie Gertie and my Aunty Rose, stayed in England, and my Father subsequently joined the Royal Navy. I knew Aunty Gertie quite well, but never met Aunty Rose, although I remember Mum referring to her quite often.

On my fifth birthday Mum came home from work with her bag bulging in an unusual way. She said that if I could tell her what was in the bag I could have it as a birthday present. I felt the bag on the outside and tried hard to guess what it was. I suddenly heard a little yap and knew immediately that it was a puppy! She took it gently out of the bag, and put a soft furry sandy and white bundle into my arms. The puppy, a nondescript mixture of breeds and obtained from a work colleague, was christened Flossie, and became my constant companion.

My Father, Percy Stanley Baker, had been in the Royal Navy for 22 years, based at Chatham in Kent. When he finished his naval service, he became an electrician with Kent Electric. I wasn't aware of the problems between my parents, in fact I remember Dad as a kind man who used to take me out of the tin bath in front of the fire, wrap me in a big towel, sit me on his lap and tell me stories. Having been in the Navy, Dad had always had his tot of rum every day. When Mum found out about this she was horrified, and her nagging probably did more to drive Dad out of the house and into the pubs than any other problem. In those days pubs were not fit places for women to go to so it never occurred to Mum to join him, especially with her intense dislike of all things alcoholic. Dad's frequent visits to the pub coupled with her inability to keep house properly became the problems on which their marriage eventually foundered after more than 18 years. I was blissfully unaware that this situation existed, and in 1947 at the age of six, I was catapulted out of my happy existence in Kent, when Mum left Dad and took my sister, then 16, me and Flossie my dog, to post-war, bomb-damaged London to live. She left my brother Peter, then 13, with Dad, as he was becoming a handful to control, getting into all sorts of mischief, and she always believed that boys "needed a father behind them".

Chapter 2 – London

Mum and Joanie both worked at the Law Courts in London and had travelled to work by train every day from Kent, so it made life a little easier for them to just have a bus ride to work. Joanie worked in the telephone exchange and Mum worked in the Divorce Courts as a secretary. For the first three weeks in London we shared a council flat in Bermondsey with a colleague of Mum's and her family, and then Mum rented the ground floor of a house in Peckham, with an additional small bedroom at the turn of the stairs up to the top floor. This was my bedroom, and Joanie and Mum shared the back bedroom downstairs. We had a front parlour and a small kitchen at the back. The only toilet was outside at the back of the house – I was scared to go out to it on my own in the dark, so Flossie would trot out beside me and wait for me outside the toilet, then accompany me back inside. Our toilet paper was newspaper cut into squares and threaded onto a string which was hung on a nail on the door … it felt very luxurious when Mum bought oranges or tangerines, as these came wrapped in a square of tissue paper and these pieces of tissue found their way onto the string too. There was a small garden with big sycamore trees dividing it from the back of the gardens behind. An elderly gentleman, Mr Butler, owned the house, an intimidating figure who always wore a long black coat and a bowler hat, and insisted that I called him Uncle Tom. I used to hear him shuffling up the stairs to his rooms at night, and I hid under the bedclothes with childish terror. He was always the perfect gentleman and never once did anything to harm me, but I still shiver when I think of him. The house was an end-of-terrace one, next to a cardboard box factory, and further down the street there were the bombed-out remains of several houses – a quite different playground to the big orchard that I was used to! The house was in Camelot Street, just off the Old Kent Road, and I went to Camelot Street Primary School. When I revisited the area many years later the whole area had sadly been torn down and rebuilt as council flats.

About a month after we left Kent there was a knock at the door. When Mum opened it, there stood my Dad with my brother. He pushed Peter forward, and said to Mum "*He's your son as well as mine, and I can't handle him, so you keep him*". With that he left, and from then on I had to share my room with Peter for the next three years. Although he teased me incessantly and constantly warned me on pain of death not to touch the fragile balsa wood and tissue paper aeroplanes that he so lovingly constructed, I didn't mind one bit – if we went out to play he was my bodyguard and protector, my absolute hero. The streets of London in those days were quite rough, and without him to stick up for me I think I would have been bullied and picked on, as I was quite small for my age. In fact, Peter affectionately christened me "Titch", and it was a nickname that all my family used for me until I left school.

I never felt 'different' for not having a Father around, as a lot of my generation had lost their Fathers in the war, so it was not an unusual situation. Until I was eight I had to be out of the house for the hours that Mum and Joanie were at work – 8.00am to 6.00pm. I never felt this was strange or unsafe, as most of my friends were also locked out until their working parents arrived home each evening. We had great adventures, exploring the bombed-out houses, probably in great danger, but we all survived and were none the worse for it. Two or three houses down from us was a big bombed out area where probably three terraced houses had stood. A carpet of hardy marigold plants had established themselves in the debris, and their cheerful yellow flowers hid the devastation beneath them. A battered old galvanised zinc water tank lay in the middle of the site with a hole on one side large enough for a child to climb through, but to us children this was no ordinary tank – it was a flying saucer, a bus, an aeroplane … anything we wanted it to be. Round the corner was another bombed-out house with the staircase still intact whilst most of the rest of the house had been blown apart. The joists which formed the middle floor were still attached to the staircase; it was a great adventure to walk up the wobbly staircase and pretend to be a tightrope walker in a circus, walking unsteadily across a beam no more than about four inches wide, about ten feet up. Heaven only knows what injuries we would have sustained had we fallen! During the school holidays Mum would give me a jam sandwich in a paper bag and a bottle of water and I, together with lots of my friends, would walk the couple of miles up to Pepys Park at New Cross and spend the whole day there happily playing games such as 'What's the time, Mr Wolf?', climbing trees and eating our jam sandwiches, which by lunch time had become quite curled at the edges. The walks there and back were big adventures, as we all believed that if you saw an ambulance or a Black Maria (the black vans used to transport prisoners), you had to hold your collar to avoid bad luck until you saw a dog – there was great competition to see who could see a dog first, and we must have looked a strange sight, a group of ragamuffins all walking along holding our collars! Flossie was my constant companion throughout all these adventures, and with Peter always there to look after me as well I knew I would be safe. I became a "latch-key kid" when I reached eight years of age; it became common to hang a key on string from the letterbox inside the door, so you could reach through the letterbox and pull the key out to the front of the door, and unlock it. It seems unbelievable now that in those days very young children were left to their own devices out on the street, and only trusted with a house key once they reached an age when they were considered to be sensible enough to be given access to the house!

The house was lit by, and we cooked on, gas but we had no bathroom, as was common in those days. Every Monday night I would meet Mum and Joanie off the bus from work and we would all walk up to the Ilderton Road Public Baths. Men and women had to use separate buildings. The bath cost sixpence per person, but Mum and I always shared a bath to save money. When your turn came you were ushered into a cubicle with a bath and some coat hooks, and a big water spout into the bath, but no control on it – the water was turned on from the outside of the cubicle by the lady Attendant. She would put hot water in to start, and then the cold. If it was still too hot, you would have to call "*More cold in No. 6, please*", and she would eventually come and add some cold water. Emerging with wet hair and shivering with the cold in the winter, we would go to buy our weekly treat – fish and chips, eaten from the newspaper on the walk home – heaven! Another treat was the Saturday morning cinema for children. Peter and I were 'ABC Minors' (a film club for the under-15's) and it used to cost tuppence to get in to the ABC Cinema for two or three hours entertainment – Abbott and Costello, the Three Stooges, Laurel and Hardy, Batman, Superman, westerns featuring Roy Rogers and his horse 'Trigger', Lassie and many other favourites. Following the films, we had an hour of community singing, and that's the reason I can still sing 'Jerusalem', 'Bless 'Em All', 'It's a long way to Tipperary', 'Land of Hope and Glory', 'There'll always be an England', the National Anthem and many other patriotic songs word-perfect. 'Sing' is perhaps too ambitious a word to use, me being totally non-musical, but I certainly remember all those words!

I had various chores to do to earn my pocket money. I had to fetch a bucket of coal up from the coal cellar every day; I had to get the towels and soap ready to take to the Public Baths each Monday; I had to go to the horse-meat stall each week to buy Flossie her meat for the week (no cans of dog food then!); and I had to keep my bedroom tidy. For these jobs I was given sixpence a week and I had no choice on how this was spent. Tuppence went into a savings tin and every three weeks Mum bought me a sixpenny National Savings stamp; tuppence was used to pay for the ABC Minors; and tuppence went into another tin to build up a fund that I could spend on birthday and Christmas presents for the family.

On Joanie's 18th birthday we all went to the ABC Cinema to see a film called 'Unknown Island'. It was about a plane that crashed on a previously undiscovered island where dinosaurs still roamed, and the people on board, all of whom survived the crash, had several hair-raising encounters with the dinosaurs. It absolutely terrified me, and when we got home we all made a beeline for the outside toilet. Fred (Joanie's boyfriend, who I adored) was pretending that the big sycamore trees in our back garden were dinosaurs to frighten us all. When it finally came to my turn to use the toilet I found myself on my own with these big looming shapes around me ... thank heaven Flossie stayed with me to keep me company!

Mum was quite an accomplished pianist, playing without any written music whatsoever; she was determined that I should learn to play properly and be able to read music, so she sent me to piano lessons one night each week. I absolutely hated them – I didn't have a musical bone in my body. The piano teacher rapped me across the knuckles with a ruler if I played a wrong note and at eight years old you soon learn to play from memory to avoid the ruler. Consequently, Mum received reasonable reports of my progress ... so the lessons continued. At the same time Mum was determined that I should learn ballet. In those days, in Peckham Rye, there was a Black

& White milk bar, and in a room above this a ballet teacher gave lessons on a Saturday afternoon, so Mum enrolled me. We would do some shopping first and Mum would buy me either a pomegranate, a liquorice stick (which looked liked a piece of wood from a tree, but when chewed produced a strong liquorice taste) or a honeycomb and I was allowed to eat this after my ballet lesson. Unfortunately, not only was I totally un-musical, I had no rhythm or natural balance either and when the owners of the milk bar complained that the heavy banging on the floor above was causing their lights to shake and flicker, a process of elimination led to the conclusion that it must be me, so Mum was politely asked to remove me! I was mortified, mainly because I loved wearing the little white tutu that Mum and Joanie had made for me. I retain to this day a love of music and ballet ... but only to listen to and to watch.

Mum eventually had to go to Court to obtain some maintenance money from Dad for Peter and myself, but he often defaulted on the payments, so life was a struggle for her financially. I was too young to realise just how difficult things were, and as my Dad would come to London about once a year to see me and Peter (Joanie refusing to have anything to do with him, as she was aware of how unfairly he was treating Mum), bringing me presents, I thought he was wonderful. Clothing, food, everything was on ration, and he used to bring his sweet ration coupons and give them to me to give to Mum. He also bought me my first watch, and a beautiful copy of "Little Women" by Louisa May Alcott that I still have to this day.

Mum was very religious, so we attended Christ Church in Old Kent Road – three times on a Sunday … Morning Prayer, Sunday School and Evensong! Mum was a Sunday School teacher, and also Tawny Owl for the Brownies, to which I belonged; Peter joined the Scouts … but not for long – being well behaved and polite was not for him! The Vicar was a wonderful gentleman called Rev. Ronald Francis, and he was loved by all his parishioners. The children all called him Uncle Ron, and he used to take us away to Summer Camp, giving the deprived children of Peckham a great holiday each year.

All this religion didn't, however, make me a better child! I never pilfered from shops but I frequently stole the odd coin or two from any money lying around in the house – I remember with shame that Peter often took the blame for it … but on one occasion I thought I had the perfect plan. Joanie had a small lockable cash box into which she put money for her holidays. I happened on the key one day whilst on school holiday when I was searching in her chest of drawers for the odd coin or two that might have slipped out of the pockets of her clothes. Triumphant, I opened the cash box to find a one pound note and some change. I took the pound note to the sweet shop round the corner in Old Kent Road, spent nearly ten shillings on the only sweets you could buy off-ration at that time – Palma Violet cachous, and chalky alphabet letters. This turned out to be an enormous amount … enough to last me weeks, I thought. When I got back home, I carefully placed the ten shilling note and a few coppers back in the cash box, thinking that Joanie wouldn't remember whether she had had a pound or a ten shilling note in there, and returned the key to its hiding place. I had an ancient hand-me-down doll's pram, styled after the Swallow prams that were so popular then with a deep recess inside the body of the pram underneath where the baby lay. My favourite doll, Ethel, lay in the doll's pram so I took her out, lifted the board that concealed the recess and stashed my loot in what I considered to be the perfect hiding place! Then I went out to play, secure in the knowledge that I could gorge on the sweets at night when I was in the bedroom before Peter came to bed. That night I was unduly keen to go to bed, and when I thought enough time had elapsed I felt around in the darkness for Ethel, quietly removed her from the pram, and prepared for a feast ... wrong!! There was nothing in the recess at all ... nothing. I tried to rack my brains to remember if I could possibly have hidden the sweets anywhere else, but all I could remember was removing Ethel and putting them all in the bottom of the pram. I lay there wondering what could have happened until my curiosity got the better of me and I went downstairs to the front room on the pretext of asking for a drink of water. I opened the door ... and there sat Mum, Joanie, Fred (Joanie's boyfriend) and Peter, all with their arms folded across their chests, glaring at me! My booty was spread out on the table in front of them, and Mum said *"We were wondering how long it would be before you came down!"*. There was no point in denying what I had done or trying to make excuses – Joanie was delegated to give me a good hiding with the dog's lead, and I went to bed suitably punished for a despicable action. However, where religion hadn't taught me that what I did was wrong, the good hiding did ... and I NEVER actually stole anything again. I discovered many years later that the shopkeeper, who knew Mum and Joanie from their regular visits to the shop for cigarettes, had called them over when they got off the bus from work and asked if it was OK for me to have a one pound note to be spending in the shop. They decided, (whilst I was out to play), to see if they could find what the shop-keeper had told them I had bought, and my hiding-place was not as perfect as I had thought. It didn't take them long to find and confiscate the sweets. I never did find out who ate the sweets, or if indeed the shop-keeper gave a refund for them.

On a regular basis, the children of Camelot Street Primary School received parcels of clothing from the children at a school in Canada, and on one such occasion I was given a really pretty yellow dress. I took it home and Mum hung it in the wardrobe to wear for best, but I decided that I wanted to wear it to school so one morning, without Mum knowing, I put it on underneath my blouse and gym slip before I left the house. When I arrived at school I went into the girls' toilets and took off the blouse and gym slip, and revelled in the admiring glances I got from the other children. The teacher, however, was not so impressed and called me out to her desk to ask why I wasn't wearing school uniform. I was surprised how glibly the lie slipped out – "*I tore my gym slip just before I was due to leave for school, and Mum didn't have time to mend it – but she will tonight*". I was told that if anything like that happened again I must bring a note with me from Mum explaining the situation. "*That was easy!*" I thought. What I wasn't expecting was the Headmaster to send a stern letter containing the same instruction to Mum! Another good hiding with the dog's lead, and another important lesson learned! Sadly, the dress eventually became a victim of the 'bagwash', a system that enabled people who had no means of washing their clothes (many of the London houses had no electricity and only an old copper for boiling whites in), where the soiled items were placed in a hessian sack, tied at the top with string and collected once a week. I am not familiar with how they actually washed the clothes, but I believe that the tied-up sacks were pushed through pipes containing hot soapy water and delivered back, soaking wet, to the house the following week when the next sackful was collected. This worked fine until, as often happened, one of the sacks contained an item coloured red or dark blue, the colour leaching out in the pipes and colouring everyone else's washing a delicate shade of pink or blue. My lovely yellow dress came back a sort of 'nappy green' colour after one such wash! I cried about it for days.

Mum made sure that we had one holiday a year, and having friends (who, out of respect, we children always addressed as 'Aunty' and 'Uncle') in Seaford in Sussex (Aunty Ethel and Uncle George); in Marston Montgomery in Derbyshire (Aunty Evelyn and Uncle Jim); and Aunty Mary who lived at Lee-on-the-Solent, near Portsmouth in Hampshire, I remember wonderful holidays – and Flossie always came with us to those areas. In the summer of 1948 when I was seven, we went to stay with Aunty Mary for a week. We spent each day on the beach, come rain or shine. The pier at Lee-on-the-Solent had been bombed during the war and the local council were dismantling it. Huge pieces of tangled, jagged metal were left on the beach for eventual removal and with the natural curiosity of a seven year old, I clambered up onto one of these girders. I slipped, felt the metal graze my left leg, climbed down and went across to Mum saying "*Look, Mummy, look what I've done*". With horror she saw the huge v-shaped gash in my calf, the muscle hanging out and blood everywhere. She scooped me up in her arms and carried me to the First Aid Post on the promenade, which turned out to be closed. A man in a red two-seater open-topped sports car said to her "*That child is badly injured; let me take her to the Doctor's.*" There was no room for Mum to get into the car so he told her to follow the car and promptly sped away. Nowadays, this would be a very risky thing to let happen to your child, but he was as good as his word and took me straight to the nearest Doctor. Mum, after searching the side streets, eventually found the red car parked outside a Doctor's surgery. The Doctor said that because of the embedded rust, the injury was too serious for him to deal with in the surgery so an ambulance was called, and Mum and I were rushed to the Casualty Department at Fareham Hospital. They told Mum that they didn't think they could save the leg and I would probably have to have it amputated from the knee down. They made Mum wait in the waiting room and then set about doing what they could for me. The Specialist decided that they wouldn't have to amputate after all, so they put 19 stitches in my leg and as it was soon after the war, there was little anaesthetic available, so I remember the experience as excruciating, screaming my head off – screams that Mum was able to hear from the Waiting Room. When it was stitched they took me out to Mum in a wheelchair with a blanket over my legs, told Mum it was all done, and that she should bring me back each day to have the dressings changed. They provided an ambulance back to Aunty Mary's, and it wasn't until the ambulance men lifted the wheelchair out of the ambulance and removed the blanket that Mum realised that I still had two legs. She passed out and had to be revived by the ambulance men! We stayed another week whilst the injury was tended daily at the hospital and then went back to London. The wound took a long time to heal as it kept getting infected, but eventually I ended up with a spectacular v-shaped scar on my leg ... and used it as an excuse ("*My leg is sore today, Miss*") to get out of sports lessons and exercise for years!

Chapter 3 – The Parting

Dad was right about one thing ... Peter was becoming a handful. He never did anything criminal, he just got into mischief. He joined a group of boys who used to hang out together on street corners, making a noise and disturbing the local populace. On one occasion they were in Peckham Rye when a rival gang started snatching handbags. Peter and his mates chased and caught two of them, holding them until the Police came. They were hailed in the local newspaper as heroes, which made me even more proud of him. However, it didn't stop him from being a general nuisance in the locality and Mum was at her wit's end, not knowing how to handle him. During one occasion when she was talking to the Vicar, Uncle Ron, about Peter, he suggested that she consider sending him to Australia under the Big Brother Movement. This was a scheme designed to assign young men, referred to as 'Little Brothers', to farms out there where they were trained in farming methods, and if they worked hard, ultimately the farmer would give them a small part of the farm to run themselves[1]. Mum investigated this possibility, (not knowing that it was not as good a scheme as it sounded) and Peter was keen on the idea, so before too much time had elapsed he was undergoing a medical examination and an interview to assess his suitability.

In January, 1950, Peter was accepted as a suitable candidate for the Big Brother Movement and was given a sailing date in May that year. The _'Daily Mirror'_ ran an article about him and about the new life that he was leaving England, and all his family, for. I was so proud that I had a 'famous' brother! He was to sail on an Orient Line (subsequently taken over by P&O) liner, the SS Otranto (20,000 tons) and disembark at Melbourne, where he was to be met by the farmer to whom he was assigned, his 'Big Brother' who owned a huge farm in New South Wales.

By this time Joanie was engaged to be married to Fred, and as my Dad refused to attend the wedding, she dearly wanted Peter to give her away at the ceremony, so the date was arranged for February 11th, 1950, a few weeks before Peter was due to sail. Fred's sister was to be Matron of Honour and I was thrilled to be told that I would be bridesmaid. Joanie was unable to afford a wedding dress or bridesmaids' dresses, but the lady who was Brown Owl to Mum's Tawny Owl in the Brownies had recently married, and she offered Joanie the use of a beautiful wedding dress and two bridesmaids' dresses. I was thrilled to bits, the dress fitted perfectly, and a feather headdress in lemon to match the dress was bought to complete the outfit. (I kept the headdress for 20 years

---

[1] This was the theory, but in reality it rarely worked out that way. The youngsters were used as 'slave labour', and, on the whole, treated very badly.

before I threw it out!). So many new things happened to me that day, I shall remember it forever! I had my hair set for the first time ever: I wore my first pair of white ... yes, white ... satin shoes, in war-torn London where every street was grubby; I went in a car for the first time (imagine that nowadays – never having been in a car before the age of eight!); I tasted wine for the first time; and I tasted wedding cake for the first time. The whole day was like a fairy tale to me, everyone was so happy. Joanie and Fred went to live with Fred's Mum, the matriarch of a Cockney family, who had a spare bedroom that they could use. Two of Fred's brothers, Sid and Bill, also lived in the house in Shorncliffe Road, off the Old Kent Road. I remember it as a happy place, with family coming and going all the time.

The wedding had faded into a lovely memory when the sad but inevitable parting with Peter happened. Mum and I went to Tilbury by train with Peter to see him off. I had never seen such a huge ship in my life! We were allowed to go on board whilst he put his luggage, two battered old cases, into the cabin he was to share with five other young men. Then the announcement came that all non-passengers had to leave the ship ... and then it hit me. What was I going to do without my hero to protect me, and when would I see him again? I sobbed and clung to him, but there was nothing for it, Mum and I had to leave the ship. We stood on the dockside and managed to pick Peter out on one of the upper decks. There were masses of paper streamers that had been thrown from the decks to the waiting friends and relatives below – the colours are still etched vividly on my mind. Then the ship sounded an eardrum-shattering horn, and started to move slowly away from the dock. Watching all those coloured streamers break broke my heart, and I dearly wished that I too could go to the faraway country that was going to become home for my beloved big brother. I was inconsolable all the way home … a home that would now seem very empty with just Mum and me in it. Most of the love and affection that I experienced as a child had come from Joanie and Peter – Mum had received precious little love from her own Mother, and she found it difficult to be demonstrative in that way. However, now it was just her and me, so a bond formed between us that was to stand us in good stead in the future.

Chapter 4 – Postcards Galore!

The first two weeks were dreadful. Peter had promised to write to us, but more importantly, to ME. Then a postcard arrived from Marseilles addressed to Mum. It was great to receive his news … but where was MY postcard? He was having a great time on board ship, had met Sid, another boy heading for the same area as he was, near Berrigan in New South Wales. They had become good friends, and it must have been reassuring for them to have each other to share this great adventure.

The next postcard arrived, from Gibraltar this time, but also addressed to Mum. By this time I had begun to believe that Peter would never send me anything, and I cried myself to sleep at night, believing he had forgotten me. He was still enjoying every minute of the trip, the weather was getting warmer and he was swimming a lot in the pool on the ship. They had crossed the Bay of Biscay in very rough weather, but Peter had not suffered the sea-sickness that some of the other passengers did, so it presented him with no problems. I suppose having a sailor for a Father helped him to get his 'sea legs' fairly quickly!

After a few days, to my great joy, a letter turned up addressed solely to me! It had been posted in Naples in Italy, and I opened it with feverish enthusiasm – he hadn't forgotten me after all. It was a long letter in which Peter told me all about life on board the ship; that Sid's full name was 'very posh' – Sidney Arthur Richards Carpenter; that the next port of call would be Port Said at the start of the Suez Canal; then they were due to call at Aden, then Ceylon; and after Ceylon there would be a 'Crossing the Line' ceremony. Not being heavily into geography, I took the letter to school with me, not least of all to show all my friends, but also to look at the school atlas and follow Peter's journey. I remember being totally impressed when I discovered that Port Said was in the north of Africa – it seemed to me that my brother was in another world. I had absolutely no idea what a 'Crossing the Line' ceremony was, and nor did my family, but my teacher said it was probably to do with crossing the Equator. She showed me the line on the map, so I felt very knowledgeable that evening when I relayed what I had learned to Mum, Joanie and Fred.

Another postcard arrived addressed to Mum, this time from Port Said. Peter was obviously enjoying himself – there were, it transpired, a few families who were emigrating on board with teenage daughters, and he and Sid made the most of the opportunity to make friends with them. When I read this, I felt a little jealous, especially as the postcard was for Mum, but she pointed out that it was just friendship, and not like being related, which made me put aside the jealousy and continue to hero-worship Peter from afar.

Mum received a long letter from Peter from Aden. He had been relaxing during the trip down the Suez Canal and had had time to write more than a postcard. The letter was full of anecdotes about the day-to-day happenings on the ship, including the sightings of flying fish (my child mind could not somehow take in this concept and I imagined fish the size of whales taking to the skies!) and the excursions that he had made at all the ports he had stopped at. He told her that he had taken photographs on the voyage, but had not been able to afford to get them developed and printed but that he would send photos as soon as he could.

Peter's next port of call was Colombo in Ceylon, which is now Sri Lanka. This time the postcard was addressed to me, a picture of a beautiful temple with a huge statue of Buddha. He said that the next part of the trip was ten days at sea until they reached Fremantle in Australia. The 'Crossing the Line' ceremony was due to take place during this time. I was entranced and amazed at the exciting adventures that my big brother was having and proudly took the postcard to school, where my teacher made me stand at the front of the class and read it out.

From Fremantle, Peter sent Mum another letter telling us all about the fun of the 'Crossing the Line' ceremony. One of the crew dressed up as Neptune with a grass skirt and a trident and other members of the crew were dressed as natives and threw all the passengers into the swimming pool. He confessed that he had drunk some beer and been less than steady on his feet – Mum, with her hatred of all things alcoholic, was infuriated by this….but what could she do, with her son thousands of miles away?!

Finally, I received a postcard from Adelaide relaying how rough it had been in the Great Australian Bight and how he and Sid had helped other passengers who were seasick. I think there was more comforting of the young ladies going on than any attention to the older passengers!

What I hadn't appreciated was that the news we were receiving from Peter was well out of date by the time we received it – letters and cards would take from about two weeks to a month to arrive. Peter had arrived in Melbourne in late June and was collected by the farmer so he was well into the Australian way of life whilst we were still reading about life on board ship. There was a long and worrying silence from him and we started to wonder if indeed he had arrived safely. We learned afterwards that the delay was because Peter was being required to work from dawn until dusk and at the end of each day he was so exhausted that all he wanted to do was sleep.

Chapter 5 – Peter in Australia

When we finally did hear, it was in the form of a long letter, with photographs, from a young man who had changed beyond all recognition from the weedy teenager who had left England some four months earlier. Peter said that he loved the life, even though it was hard work. He was riding a lot, but the biggest new interest in his life was Lorraine, the daughter of the farmer he worked for. Now I was really jealous! The photographs showed him with her, laughing, swimming and generally enjoying each other's company. He had developed into a handsome, muscled Adonis, and my adoration for him increased tremendously.

Even though they were few and far between, the arrival of Peter's letters was always an exciting time for me, hearing all about his new life. Looking back, I believe he was missing us, his family, quite a lot, as there crept into his letters a few comments to Mum about *'what a wonderful country this is, and why don't you bring Dorothy out here?'* We were to learn much later that he actually hated the life on the farm, he was poorly paid and worked hard all the daylight hours, but his friendship with Lorraine made it bearable. He was given his food and a roof over his head (in the form of the shearer's accommodation – basic dormitories with a cold tap and canvas over the window and door openings, only used by shearer's during the shearing season), but the only way he could get spend money was to ride the boundary fences, made from barbed wire, and if any sheep had got caught on the fence and died, Peter was entitled to sell the fleece for anything he could get for it. Some of the sheep had been dead for days, so large was the boundary of the farm, and some of the bodies were heaving with flies and maggots but he learned to deal with that in order to get some pocket money for himself. Peter added that, as he rode his horse, his thighs would be black with flies, and with one slap he could kill dozens of them … and yes, he did wear the typical swaggie's hat with the bobbing corks hanging down to keep flies off his face. His pleas to Mum obviously hit a chord in her and, although I didn't realise it at the time, she made enquiries at Australia House to see if they would accept her and me as emigrants. At that time, Australia was desperate to attract qualified people out there, and the cost to the emigrant was just £10 for the trip – for a child under 14 it was free. All the emigrant needed was a job to go to …

Joanie and Fred were not too happy about Mum's decision, but they recognised that it would give us both the opportunity of a better life. Their own prospects were not that brilliant, living with Fred's Mum in post-war Britain. Fred was a lift installation foreman with Evans Lifts and Joanie still worked as a telephonist at the Law Courts so they had a reasonable joint income but very little chance of owning their own property in the foreseeable future. It would take many years of saving for them to be able to afford the required deposit. The reconstruction of the bomb-damaged buildings in London was slow to start, and it was the norm for newly-weds to spend several years living with in-laws before renting or buying a place of their own.

Late in 1950 I found myself with Mum in Australia House undergoing interviews and medicals. We both passed with no problems and with Mum's secretarial skills, she was accepted as a suitable candidate but she had to be sponsored by someone who would be willing to employ her. This presented her with a problem, as she knew no-one in Australia except my brother and he was in no position to find her a job … or was he? Peter spoke to the farmer he worked for, who told Peter that he had a brother who was also a farmer, 50 miles away just outside of Corowa in New South Wales, who was in desperate need of a housekeeper as he had three young children and his wife was expecting their fourth child. Peter wrote to Mum, very excited to be able to solve the employment problem for her. The farmer's brother was contacted; he filled in the appropriate forms and was accepted as a sponsor.

One of the most distressing aspects of this big adventure for me was that I had to part with Flossie. Aunty Ethel and Uncle George in Seaford, Sussex, volunteered to have her so we spent a sad weekend down there saying good-bye to Flossie. I knew deep down that she would have a wonderful home with lots of walks across the Sussex Downs and Aunty Ethel's wonderful cooking for food, but I felt that I was having part of me amputated. We had been constant companions for 5 years and I knew I would miss her dreadfully.

Mum realised that she would only be able to take a limited amount of luggage to Australia, so she set about disposing of all the things that she would be unable to take. The Kidd Family Bible was one of those things and also the silver-plated epergne that was presented to my Grandfather by Horlicks on his retirement – how sad she was at parting with the only mementoes of her beloved Father. We had one metal sea-chest with a big handle at each end, a remnant of my Father's time in the Royal Navy, and oddly, she filled this with woollen articles … cardigans, knitted and crocheted dresses, skirts and tops – would we be needing these in a hot country? She also managed to squeeze in some small books, and thankfully some photograph albums containing wonderful sepia photographs of her parents and herself as a child – which I still have to this day. Apart from that, we were allowed one personal case each, so we carefully selected the clothes to cover both cold and hot weather that we wanted to take with us on board.

Early in 1951, Mum and I were given March 22nd as our departure date, and we were to sail on the SS Orion (23,300 tons), another Orient Line ship (all their ship's names began with an 'O'), from Tilbury Docks in London, arriving in Melbourne on 23rd April, 1951. I remember being relieved that we were not sailing with the P&O line, as I had heard the adults talking about a rumour that if you got up early on board and crossed the decks where the religious crew members were praying, they would knife you – it was only a silly rumour, of course, but it terrified me to think about it!

I was just ten years old, and ecstatic with the prospect of seeing Peter again and setting out on an adventure that would rival his …

… and so began a period in my life that warrants setting down on paper, if only to explain to my children and grandchildren what makes me tick!

Part Two

The Journey

Chapter 6 – Much Excitement!

Although I had talked incessantly at school about the fact that we were going to Australia, I don't really think that my friends actually believed me. However, it came to my last day at school and the teacher asked me to come to the front of the class. She presented me with an Enid Blyton book and asked the class to give me three cheers and wish me well. I was so proud that I was the one who was going on this big adventure. My friend Jean Pettitt promised to write to me and I skipped all the way home from school that day, so happy was I that at last they believed what I had been saying all along.

A few days later, Joanie and Fred accompanied us by train to Tilbury and came on board with us just as Mum and I had done with Peter ten months previously. We had been allocated a six-berth cabin and on taking our cases down, we met the four girls – Pam, Margaret, Cissy and Ann – who were to be our cabin-mates for the next month. They were all young working-class girls, eager to start their new life. We went up on deck with Joanie and Fred and this time the parting was even more emotional than the parting with Peter had been, especially for Mum. They left the ship, the horn sounded and the thousands of coloured streamers again made a huge impression on me as they broke, one by one, as the ship pulled away from the dock.

Mum and I immediately set about exploring the ship. We had been advised that we must not go anywhere near the First Class area, except when the ship was docked at a port, when we would be allowed to use the First Class swimming pool … an odd rule, but it was rarely taken advantage of because we had a perfectly adequate pool in Economy Class. I had no idea that there could be such luxury on a ship. The restaurants, decks, leisure and recreational areas were all spacious and pleasant. However, the cabin was cramped with very little storage space, so we had to be considerate and tidy all the time. The cabin was on the lowest deck of all; a strong smell of diesel from the engine room accompanied us throughout the voyage because the porthole was permanently closed as in rough weather it was below sea-level. The bathroom was along the corridor a little way, and the baths always used sea water, leaving your hair and body sticky afterwards – never mind, we got used to it. Our cabin steward was very dishy, much to the delight of the four girls we were sharing with. Our bunks got made every day and the cleaning and washing was done for us, so it felt quite luxurious.

We had been advised of the number of our table in one of the dining rooms and we had been allocated the first sitting – all six of us from our cabin were allocated the same table, but you were allowed to change tables once the journey had started to if you wanted to, although you had to stick with the same sitting. The food was basic but good ... and I tasted banana for the first time ever at our first meal on board. In one of the lounges there was a notice board advising us of the events that would be taking place on board during the coming week; when we needed to put our clocks forward, an hour at a time; there was also information about whist drives, bridge games, Church services, films in the cinema, deck quoits and deck tennis competitions, a tote on the number of nautical miles travelled in the last 24 hours (which I actually won once, a few shillings to swell my spend money, which came from all my National Savings stamps that Mum cashed in for me), dances, shows and deck drills. Deck drills happened every week, and you had to don the life jacket issued to you on the first day, and congregate by your allocated life-boat whilst your names were ticked off on a list. Those passengers who didn't take this seriously were severely reprimanded by the Officer in Charge and by the second week, **everyone** attended punctually! There was also information on the ports that we were due to call at, and the excursions available at those ports.

I slept well the first night but woke up feeling slightly queasy. I managed to make it to the dining room but the smell of food sent me straight back down to the cabin to lie down. Here was I expecting to get involved in all sorts of competitions and ending up in bed on the first day! The cabin steward, Bob, came in to make the bunks, and feeling sorry for me, he brought me an orange in case I got hungry. I dozed off to sleep, woke feeling slightly better, so I tucked into the orange and tried to go back to sleep. The orange was a bad move, as within a few minutes I was dashing down the corridor to the bathroom and was very, very seasick; the diesel fumes didn't help either. It was absolutely dreadful, and made me feel like I wanted to die. I crept back to my bunk and spent the rest of the day there, feeling very sorry for myself. Mum, on the other hand, had never been affected with seasickness so she enjoyed every minute of the first whole day on board. We had crossed the Bay of Biscay in quite a heavy storm and I was not the only one to succumb. The following day I woke up, expecting to feel the same but, miraculously, I felt much better and was soon back to normal.

There was a buzz of excitement going around Economy Class. Someone let slip that we had some celebrities on board, in First Class. The singer Evelyn Laye was one of them; also on board was the Australian comedian, Bill Kerr, later well known for his comedy shows with Tony Hancock. He was accompanying his Mother back to Australia – rumour had it that she was quite fond of a little tipple now and again. Apparently, when we were in the Bay of Biscay, she had fallen and broken her leg, so we didn't see much of her for the rest of the voyage. Evelyn Laye, however, sang at several of the concerts on board and was loved by all; Bill Kerr also entertained during the voyage. The big excitement, though, was because Lord and Lady Mountbatten were on board travelling to Gibraltar for an official visit. I caught occasional glimpses of the couple; I thought that Lady Mountbatten was the most elegant lady I had ever seen, and Lord Mountbatten the most handsome man. We were not allowed to leave the ship at Gibraltar (as it was not a scheduled stop) but Lord and Lady Mountbatten (he in his white naval uniform, and she in a fashionable skirt suit) disembarked in the early hours of the morning and at least three-quarters of the passengers were up to see the pomp and ceremony as they left the ship on a boat manned by smart naval crew in their white uniforms, and welcomed formally by Gibraltar, complete with fireworks. All this was a lot to take in for a 10-year old!

Life settled into a very enjoyable routine. Every morning at 10am, beef tea and crackers were served in one of the lounges. The officers and crew were in navy blue at this stage, but when we reached warmer climes they changed into their white uniforms and served us with ice cream plus the obligatory salt tablet to replace what we lost through perspiration. There were all sorts of great things to do and I loved every minute of it. I quickly became adept at deck quoits and swam every day with Mum in the salt-water swimming pool. We looked forward with excitement to arriving at our first port of call.

Chapter 7 – Port Said

Our first scheduled stop was at Port Said at the start of the Suez Canal. I looked in wonder at the great statue of Ferdinand de Lesseps at the entrance to the Canal – he was the builder and developer of the Suez Canal, which opened in 1869 and provided a sea link between the Mediterranean and the Gulf of Suez. I learned later that he was also the man who presented the Statue of Liberty to the American nation in 1884. After we anchored there were swarms of 'bum-boats' around the ship selling all sorts of fruit, lengths of fine silks, shawls, leather goods and other souvenirs. They would throw a rope up to us with a basket at its end, then send the goods up in the basket for us to inspect. For a few cigarettes, or very little money, you could buy a treasure trove. There were some unscrupulous passengers on board who just untied the rope and threw it back down, keeping the articles for nothing. The (mainly) young boys in the 'bum-boats' were not allowed on board, so there was nothing they could do about it, but there were notices on all the notice boards asking passengers not to do this. We didn't buy anything from the 'bum-boats' at Port Said, but it was fascinating watching all the bargaining going on. Mum decided not to book an organised trip, so together with our four cabin mates, we each took a rickshaw – pulled by a muscle-bound Arab youth – to the local market. What an eye-opener! There was everything imaginable on sale. There were many of the items that were being sold from the 'bum-boats', plus a whole host of other souvenirs such as carved elephants and camels, wooden figures, carved wooden chests and much more. It was just like an Aladdin's Cave. There were camels galore, donkeys being ridden by elderly wizened old men, and all the locals dressed in Arab clothing and looking like the Sheiks that I had seen in the old silent movies that I watched at the ABC Minors. I had a difficult time taking it all in, but it brought to life all the things that Peter had described in his letters and cards. First Mum bought me a big coloured woven raffia hat, essential in so much heat, then she decided I needed some new shorts so at a clothes stall she selected a couple of pairs for me and, horror of horrors, insisted that I try them on there and then! I shuffled out of the ones I had on and stood there in my panties, feeling conspicuous and dying with embarrassment ... but strangely enough, no-one took any notice. The hustle-bustle of the market just carried on around me, much to my relief. The shorts were really pretty, fitted perfectly and so not wanting to disrobe again, even though no-one had paid any attention, I insisted on keeping them on.

We eventually made our way back to the ship by rickshaw again and when back on board we compared our purchases with some of the other passengers. It was quite funny to find that some had been completely overcharged for identical articles, but on the whole the six of us from our cabin had found real bargains. The girls had bought beautiful silk shawls, some carved wooden elephants, and some embroidered silk pyjamas. I fell in love with these pyjamas but knew that we couldn't afford anything like that, so I put that dream to one side.

The ship set sail sedately down the Suez Canal, through the Great Bitter Lake about half way down the Canal and on to Suez on the edge of the Gulf of Suez. I was fascinated by the scenery on either side – there were palm trees; huts constructed of wood and corrugated iron; camel trains; and donkeys working in patches of cultivated land. Every so often there was a station which had a sign in large letters showing where we were, a big clock showing the local time, and how far along the Canal we were. We passed other large liners going in the opposite direction, which at night looked like fairy palaces all lit up. I was fully into the deck quoits and deck tennis competitions at this point, and when Mum played whist, I would sit at a table and use a pack of cards to tell people's fortunes. There were Housey-housey games (now more commonly known as Bingo), colouring competitions, children's entertainers, swimming competitions … in fact, plenty to keep any ten year old occupied and happy.

We reached the other end of the Canal and tied up at Suez. More 'bum-boats' swarmed around us and this time Mum decided to buy a leather pouffé with a brightly coloured decorated pattern on it. (Mum actually kept this and used it for the rest of her life!). She paid the equivalent of five shillings (25p) for it – in those days

Australia still used the British system of pounds, shillings and pence, so we had not needed to mentally convert our money into a different currency, but the 'bum-boats' would accept anything, even cigarettes, in payment. It was very exciting, hauling the basket containing our purchase up the side of the ship. Mum inspected it, made sure that the zip underneath it worked alright (some didn't!) and sent the money back down in the basket.

We were not able to disembark at Suez as the ship had only stopped there to refuel, and pick up and drop off mail. We set sail through the Gulf of Suez and into the Red Sea. This is where I first noticed the porpoises that appeared round the ship, diving joyfully in and out of the waves at the bows. Also, one of the big questions in my head was finally answered – we saw flying fish. They were definitely not the size of whales, as I had at first imagined, but delicately small and glowing with all the colours of the rainbow as they caught the sunlight … and they definitely did fly! Not very high out of the water, but they seemed to rise silently from the water in great numbers, glide effortlessly about a foot above the surface and enter the water again with barely a splash. I loved to watch them, they were so beautiful. The Red Sea was calm, and the ship continued with hardly any rolling, which made swimming in the pool much less energetic, not having to keep up with the swell of the waves that we experienced in the Bay of Biscay sloshing the water from side to side.

Chapter 8 – Aden and Ceylon

We finally completed the journey down the Red Sea and anchored off Steamer Point, Aden. The small boat that ferried passengers to and from the port bustled busily back and forth and the six of us decided to leave the ship and just go for a walk around the town, operating on the assumption that there was safety in numbers. It felt strange walking on terra firma at first – we had obviously got our 'sea-legs' and were more used to the rolling motion of the ship than dry land. The local children seemed very poor, but they were all laughing happily, seemingly without a care in the world. We noticed that a lot of them had pierced ears, something we hadn't seen before on such young children. The roads were manic, with rickshaws and decorated lorries, a few cars, and lots of bicycles, so crossing the road became a challenge. The shops were nothing like the shops we knew from England, they were mainly huts constructed of anything they could find … tea chest wood figured very large, with "Finest Assam Tea" stamped all over the walls of a workshop where a man sat outside with a crude lathe worked by his feet, turning coffee table legs. The finished articles were displayed alongside him, with very beautiful, ornate, carved and inlaid tops. There were stalls selling fruit, spices and lengths of silk. I was delighted with all the new things I was seeing, often thinking of my school friends in London and how much I would have enjoyed sharing these experiences with them. I sent a postcard showing an Arab man on a camel to Jean Pettitt, but there was not enough room on the card for all my exciting news!

We returned to the ship and watched the preparations for sailing on to Ceylon. The gangway was hauled up and secured on the deck. The ship was tied up with huge ropes to massive bollards on the quay and it took several of the dock crew to release them all. The ropes would then all be coiled up neatly on the decks where passengers were not allowed to go, but visible from the deck above. The ship would sound its horn and then the pilot ship would guide the huge liner out of the harbour, making sure it was safely on its way.

I have to confess that I was getting more and more excited about seeing Peter again. We had not heard from him for quite some time and I missed his letters. I sent him a postcard from Aden telling him about my adventures and Mum wrote him a long letter, too, but we were not certain whether they would actually reach him ... not knowing how reliable the Aden post service was. Anyway, she gave him our date of arrival – we were to disembark at Melbourne on 22nd April 1951 and we hoped he would be there to meet us.

Our next port of call was Colombo in Ceylon, now Sri Lanka. Mum decided to book a guided tour for us both, so we left the ship and boarded a ramshackle old coach with open sides where the windows should have been and wooden bench-type seats. We set off through the most beautiful scenery, lush vegetation and palm trees, with happy children waving to us in the small villages we went through. Mum was keen to take some photographs of them, so when we stopped for a drink (cups of tea bought from a roadside stall – using boiled water of course, the only safe drink as their tap water was not recommended), she took some photographs. The next thing that happened was quite scary … she was surrounded by children with their hands out asking for money for allowing their photographs to be taken – but what was more alarming is that their parents joined in the general jostling and demanded that they be paid. Mum was rescued by the coach driver who advised her not to give any of them money or they would all demand it, She was quite shaken by the experience and took her photographs more discreetly after that. We trundled on, stopping at temples now and again, also a tea plantation where we were shown the tea producing process from planting to teapot, and given lunch. This consisted of some meat in a fruity sauce, and dessert of all the tropical fruits you could imagine – bananas, papaya, melon, oranges, pineapple and apricots are the ones I remember. Most of them I had never seen before. After lunch we all returned to the coach, most of the passengers perspiring profusely in the humid climate. As we had reached the hotter countries on our voyage, Mum had started to suffer quite badly with the heat, complaining frequently of headaches and tiredness. On this particular day she seemed to be suffering quite a lot, particularly as she was still affected by the confrontation with the children and their parents. However, our next stop made us both sit up and take notice – here in front of us, surrounded by palm trees and seemingly in the middle of nowhere, was the huge statue of Buddha that had appeared on the postcard that Peter had sent me all that while ago. I stood open-mouthed in front of it – I had never seen anything like it before, it was so impressive. It made the whole uncomfortable trip worthwhile. The temple nearby, screened by lush vegetation, was stunning too and I talked of nothing else as we bumped our way back to the ship. Before we went on board I bought a postcard of the Buddha – the same photograph that Peter had sent to me – wrote it and posted it to him, telling him how thrilled I was to have seen it too. We were able to buy stamps from the Purser's Office on board and post our mail in a box on the Reception Desk, but how and when it would be dealt with remained a mystery to me. However, I do know that all the mail we posted, including cards and letters to Joanie and Fred, actually did arrive eventually at their destinations.

Chapter 9 – 'Water, water everywhere, and not a drop to drink'

Notices on board advised us that the next leg of the journey would be ten consecutive days at sea with no ports to call at, but we would be celebrating the 'Crossing the Line' ceremony and also anchoring off the Cocos Islands to deliver and receive mail. The days on board seemed endless with nothing to see but sea, but the activities continued, lots of whist and bridge was played in the salons, and the children on board were kept fully entertained with clowns, magic shows, and films ... it almost felt like being back with the ABC Minors – only without the community singing! Then, after about 3 days out of Colombo we had the 'Crossing the Line' ceremony, an event that I had been eagerly awaiting since we set sail. Now I would know what it was all about! At 2pm, everyone gathered around the pool, excitedly awaiting the arrival of King Neptune. A tall, sun-tanned figure arrived, his hair an unruly mess with a headband made from sea shells, he was dressed in a skirt made from seaweed, he was painted with all sorts of scrolled symbols on his cheeks, arms and body, and he carried a huge trident. He was followed by about a dozen 'maidens' played by other crew members dressed in grass skirts and wearing long blonde wigs and a pair of half-coconuts tied across their hairy chests! The first two 'maidens' carried a large bowl, a shaving brush and a huge wooden cut-throat razor. At first we all thought that King Neptune was going to get a shave, but the rest of the 'maidens' fanned out and grabbed the onlooking men round the pool, took them over to King Neptune and made them kiss his feet, then they were forcibly held down on a chair, smothered with foam and 'shaved' by the maidens. When the mock shaving was finished, they were thrown unceremoniously into the pool, pausing only to remove watches and other valuables as quickly as they could before they got a soaking. No-one escaped their attention, except those who knew what to expect from previous journeys, and these cowards watched from the deck overlooking the pool, refusing to come down even when commanded to do so by King Neptune! We females thought that this was the end of the fun and were shocked to be similarly grabbed, put over the shoulder of a burly 'maiden', taken to the feet of King Neptune, and allowed to give him a peck on the cheek! We were not submitted to the indignity of being 'shaved' … but we were dumped unceremoniously into the pool. Fortunately Mum and I had our swimming costumes on, but some of the ladies had dresses on and were not best pleased, but the notices advertising the ceremony did say 'you will be welcomed into the wet world of King

Neptune', so it didn't take much to work out that there would be water involved! The whole event was finished off by rum punch and cakes being served on deck, and everyone agreed what wonderful fun it had all been – no wonder Peter had enjoyed it so much.

A few more days passed with endless seas, broken only by the occasional sight of another ship travelling in the opposite direction. Eventually we stood on deck and could see tiny islands with palm-fringed beaches in the distance, which gradually got larger until we were anchored off the largest of them. We were unprepared for what happened next. A huge water-tight barrel was launched overboard, and a race began from the shore to see who could reach the barrel first. There were all sorts of craft, including canoes each paddled by six men in native costumes, paddling for all they were worth; sailing boats with sails a-billowing; small canoes with one or two men in; even a raft set out from land ... but no motor-driven craft, as these were not allowed. The first boat to reach the barrel was a small yacht, and the sailors on it hauled the barrel on board, cheering with delight. We discovered that this was a tradition of the Orient Line ships and they always presented the winners with a barrel of beer – apparently rum was the drink of the islands, and good old draught beer was hard to come by, so it was a much sought-after reward for the winner of a hard-fought race. The beer barrel was duly launched overboard, and the winners fished it out of the sea, and were then followed back to the shore by all the other craft amid much cheering and celebratory noise. No doubt the inhabitants were very pleased to be receiving their long-awaited mail, and the whole island seemed to be joining in the celebrations. I have no doubt that the barrel of beer did not last long! Whilst all this was going on, a motor launch came round the back of the ship, and a small gangway was lowered to enable a couple of crew members to take a similar barrel on board containing the mail from the Cocos Islands to the rest of the world. Apparently the Orient Line ships continued this tradition for many years, and provided the only link that this little Australian colony had with the outside world.

After a few more days of endless sea, there was a real feeling of excitement on board. There was going to be a Landfall Dinner the night before we docked at Fremantle, the first port of call in Australia. Some people would be disembarking here, as the jobs they were going to were in Perth, near Fremantle or other locations in Western Australia. Mum and I were up on deck before the meal that night and we saw another huge liner approaching, lit up from top to bottom. It seemed to be coming a lot closer than most of the other ships we had seen, so we watched with fascination as the two ships passed each other. There were lots of people up on the decks on this ship, which was one of the Orient Line ships, I think the SS Ormonde, and they seemed to have their hands clasped round their mouths, shouting something. We strained to hear what they were saying and when they were exactly level with us, the message came across loud and clear – "You're going the wrong way!". What could they mean? We put it to the back of our minds, hoping that the Captain hadn't read the compass wrong, and went down to a sumptuous banquet to say farewell to those leaving the ship at Fremantle. There was the presentation of all the prizes for the competitions that had been taking place on board and I was proud to receive the Mixed Doubles Winners Prize for deck quoits, which I had won together with a 16 year-old boy James who I had been teamed up with at the start of the tournament. We both won crisp 10 shilling notes, an absolute fortune to me as I had spent most of my savings during the voyage. It was quite an emotional evening, because friendships had been made on board, some of which I am sure are still strong. Maybe there were eventually marriages as a result of these friendships, who knows? All we knew was that we would be saying goodbye to some nice people and we wished them well for their new life in this land of milk and honey that we had all chosen for ourselves.

Chapter 10 – Fremantle, Adelaide and Melbourne

The next day we stood on deck and watched the sailors tie the ship up to the quay. Then those who were leaving the ship disembarked. Everyone seemed to be brimming with anticipation and we were impatient to get going on the last few days of our journey. The six of us from our cabin decided to do some exploring, so we left the ship and had a look round Fremantle. We looked in wonder at the clean, beautiful city, with lovely buildings and an air of calm and contentment about it. We went to look at The Round Tower, which was the original prison where the first 75 British convicts sent to Fremantle were held. We stopped for lunch at a restaurant (the first proper one I had ever been in) and were blown away by how expensive it was – a lesson learned, but we enjoyed it nevertheless. I was unaware that Mum was getting short of money at this point, so it really was a blow to her to have to pay for an expensive meal, but she had the prospect of earning money when we got to the farm we were heading for when we disembarked at Melbourne, so I think she took comfort from that. We headed back to the ship, feeling that Australia really was the Utopia we had imagined it to be. That night we set sail for Adelaide, our penultimate stop. We crossed the Great Australian Bight in a heavy storm, but though many people were seasick again, fortunately my 'sea-legs' didn't let me down and I wasn't afflicted like I had been in the Bay of Biscay ... after all, I **was** a sailor's daughter!

More people were leaving the ship at Adelaide, so there were more farewells to be said. The six of us again disembarked and went to look around another beautiful city. Everywhere seemed so fresh and new compared to war-torn London and the people all looked well-dressed and prosperous. This time we bought a sandwich from a street stall ... no more expensive restaurants for us! The original Adelaide was designed to fit into a square mile and a lot of thought had gone into the planning of it. There were broad streets and lots of public parks and open spaces. It was built originally to accommodate the first free settlers to Australia and extended outwards as the population gradually increased. We caught the tram to Glenelg, one of the lovely suburbs, and wandered around shops stocked with items that we had been unable to obtain in England ... and none of them on ration! Reluctantly we made our way back to the ship to complete the very last leg of our journey. There was a message waiting for Mum in the cabin – please could she go to the Purser's Office. It turned out to be a message from her prospective employer to say that he was unable to pick us up until 24th April, the day after we docked at Melbourne. Mum was concerned, as she had very little money and would not be able to afford an overnight stay, but the Purser was very kind, and said that, as the ship was staying at Melbourne overnight, we could stay on board for the extra night. Mum was so relieved she burst into tears when we got back to the cabin. The girls were booked into the Travellers' Aid hostel in Melbourne, so they suggested that we spend the spare day with them in Melbourne sightseeing. Mum agreed, provided it didn't cost too much!

The journey to Melbourne was uneventful, and the girls and Mum and I started packing, and saying goodbye to the many friends we had made on board. Although friendships between the crew and passengers were frowned upon, each of the girls had formed a strong bond with a crew member, so fond farewells were said all round. The girls were all disembarking at Melbourne and there was a special meal served the night before we arrived, followed by a spectacular show, making our last evening together a memorable one. I was bursting with excitement at the prospect of seeing Peter again and at the new life about to start for Mum and me. The following morning we watched from the deck as the ship tied up in the port of Melbourne. I scanned the quay for any sign of Peter, but he did not appear. The port area looked a bit seedy to me, after beautiful Adelaide and Fremantle, but I was soon to learn that Melbourne was also a stunning city. Mum left a message at the Purser's Office for Peter, should he turn up, but I think she knew deep down that there was only a slim chance he would be able to make it. We had to wait whilst the girls' luggage was unloaded, and then we took two taxis – my first ever ride in a taxi – to the hostel. The girls refused to let Mum contribute to the fare, as they would have needed two taxis anyway. Once at the hostel the girls unloaded their luggage and then we all took a tram to the Botanical Gardens, the War Memorial, and the Museum. What a wonderful day that was, I was thrilled with everything I saw. The streets were very, very wide, with trams running up and down the centre of them. I was to learn many years later that the reason for this width was that from day one Melbourne had been a busy port, and early on most of the goods were transported to and from Melbourne by bullock train ... therefore the streets developed from wide tracks that enable the bullock trains to turn round without unhitching. This resulted in a fine city with broad tree-lined streets with an airy, spacious atmosphere about it. The girls decided that they wanted to visit Luna Park, the big funfair, so we took the tram there, and my eyes opened ever wider at the noise, the lights, the loud music, and the rides – I had never seen anything like it in my life. Mum told me that she could only afford one ride, and that I could choose which one. I chose the Ferris Wheel – the view from the top was magnificent and I began to feel like I was in the middle of a dream.

Sadly we made our way back to the hostel and said a very tearful farewell to the girls. We exchanged addresses and promised to keep in touch, then we caught the tram back to the docks area. The Purser had told Mum that we had to be off the ship by 10am the next morning so we went to bed for the last time in our bunks, in what suddenly seemed a very empty cabin. Fortunately we had got on so well with the girls that we had all coped with the cramped conditions with no real problems – we now missed them, it seemed so quiet without their chatter.

We were up early the next morning, had a substantial breakfast and followed the porters with our sea chest and our cases down the gangway. They put them in the shade on the quayside – we sat on them waiting, not knowing what time the farmer would turn up. Mum was very quiet and I'm sure she was wondering if she, at 51 years old, had done the right thing bringing her ten year old daughter to a strange country on the other side of the world. About an hour later, the ship left the port escorted by tugs and a pilot vessel for the last leg of her journey up the coast to Sydney. We watched with a tinge of sadness as the ship that we had called home for the last month slowly disappeared over the horizon. It seemed strange to be watching all this from the shore and not the deck. As we waited, the sun moved round and we were no longer in the shade. Although April was autumn in Australia, the noonday sun was very hot, so we had to keep moving to keep in the shade until there was no shade left. We played 'I Spy' to pass the time away and watched another great liner dock, disgorging its passengers, some of them looking somewhat nervous, some obviously full of cheerful anticipation at this brave new world that they were about to become a part of. If Mum was worried, she didn't show it. At about 2.30pm a grey station wagon pulled up and out got a man of about 45 in a checked shirt and jeans. He came across to us and asked if we were the Bakers and having introduced himself to us, he loaded all our luggage into the back of the car and we set out on our journey.

PHOTOS

1940. Mum and Dad

1947. Me aged six, just after moving to London.

1950. This picture of Peter appeared in the 'Daily Mirror' in an article about him going to Australia under the 'Big Brother Movement'. (Photo courtesy of the 'Daily Mirror')

1949. My ballet lessons didn't last long!

1951. 'Flossie' when we left her in Sussex with Aunty Ethel and Uncle George.

1951. 'Bum-boats' at Aden.

1951. Me in a rickshaw in Port Said.

1951. Me on the SS Orion en route to Australia.

1951. Mum outside the garage we were obliged to live in because no-one in Australia would give us accommodation.

1951. Mum's Brownie Pack at Corowa. I am in the middle of the back row.

1952. Me with 'Pash' near our bird cages outside the garage that we lived in.

1952. Corowa Primary School, Sixth Class. I am fourth from the left in the back row, wearing my 'Joseph' cardigan! Brenda is fourth from the right in the front row. (Photo courtesy of S. J. Campbell)

1952. Mum in her Brown Owl uniform, Peter in his Australian Army uniform, and me in my Girl Guide uniform – outside the garage that we lived in. By this time we had installed a second window in the garage.

1953. Corowa Intermediate High School, Year 1BC. I am fifth from the left in the back row of girls. Brenda is third from the right in the same row. (Photo courtesy of S. J. Campbell)

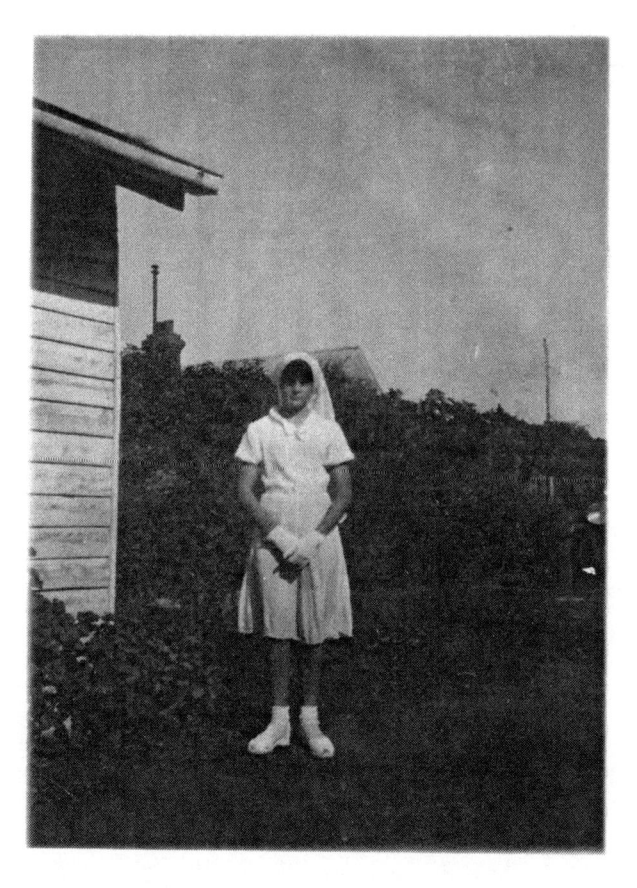

1953. Confirmation on 30th April.

*1953. Aunty Cora and Uncle Duff's
house, showing the white swan.*

*1953. The run-down council house in King Street. 'The place
you walk through' was near the chimney between the two gabled
parts of the building*

1953. Joanie and Peter at Mt. Buffalo.

1953. Joyce Rolton and me on top of the eucalyptus branches on the farm near Bendigo.

1953. Me proudly showing off my 'new' bicycle just after Joanie and Fred had returned to England.

1953. The Duke of Edinburgh's hand, taken on 5th March at Benalla by Mum when the Queen and Prince Philip visited Australia.

1953. Joy Miller and me laying the wreath at The Monument on Anzac Day, 25th April.

1953. My handsome brother Peter, aged 20

1954. 'Pash' shortly before he got run over.

1954. Brenda, Leonie Poidevin and myself on my 13th birthday in the garden at King Street. The 'dunny' can be seen at the end of the garden

Part Three

Australia

Chapter 11– The Sheep Farm

Mum's new employer explained that he had a large sheep farm ten miles outside the small town of Corowa, on the New South Wales/Victoria border. He had four children, (two of whom were about my age plus a toddler) and the baby that was due when he first said he would sponsor Mum had by this time arrived, another son just a few months old. He told us that Corowa was about 200 miles from Melbourne, so we were in for a long drive. I remained quiet, as I was told from an early age that 'children should be seen and not heard', but I was fascinated by what looked like water on the road ahead and, on reaching that point, I was astonished to see that the road was completely dry. This turned out to be a mirage – so great was the heat on the tarmac that it created this effect. I also noticed how red and sandy the soil was, quite different to England's brown soil.

Mum asked the farmer about Peter, but he bluntly replied "*He's my brother's problem; I have nothing to do with that*". This made Mum wonder why he had used the word 'problem', as she had not had the slightest clue from Peter that there might be a 'problem', but she was too polite to question her new employer further. He then outlined the duties expected of Mum as Housekeeper and even though I was only ten, it sounded like hard work to me! She was to start at 6am every morning, and her first task each day would be to go out into the farm land to gather wood for the big wood-burning range in the kitchen, enough to keep it lit all day. Then she would have to cook breakfast, lunch and tea for all the family, and fit in round that all the washing and ironing and "*of course, keep the house clean*". In addition to that, she would be expected to keep the shearers' accommodation clean when they were there (this was seasonal, so not a continuous responsibility) and finally, to babysit when required. She would have one day off a week on Sundays, and she would receive two pounds ten shillings a week in wages, the first payment being at the end of the first week. Mum went very quiet at this point and the rest of the journey was completed almost in silence, with the farmer occasionally pointing out places of interest along the route. One thing that made me sit up and take notice was a large area of blackened trees and grass, which he explained was the result of a recent bush fire which fortunately had been brought under control.

The landscape that we passed through was very brown and very dry, with many lovely old gum trees along the roadside. I eagerly scanned the horizon for kangaroos, these strange native creatures that I had heard people talk about on the ship. I didn't see any but I was too shy to ask the farmer where they were. The houses that we passed seemed quite large, but quite ramshackle to me, being built mainly of horizontal wooden slats called weatherboarding, with corrugated iron roofs. There were very few houses built of brick, but most of the houses had brick chimneys. Occasionally there would be a charred chimney stack standing on its own, the remnant of a property fallen victim to a bush fire sometime in the past. The fences were largely wire netting on wooden posts, topped with barbed wire and it seemed an enormous distance from one house to the next one. Most homesteads had a paddock at the side with horses in it and there were many, many sheep in the fields.

We finally arrived at the farm, and the family came out to greet us. The farmer's wife was a chubby lady, and she carried the baby in her arms. The three children stood shyly behind her, and I stood equally shyly behind Mum. I noticed that the front garden was full of fruit trees, but the trees were totally unlike our orchard in Kent. There were orange, lemon, grapefruit, peach and apricot trees, and some that I didn't recognise. One was a sort of pear shaped fruit, very furry, which I learned was quince, and another had small orange-coloured fruit, which was a kumquat. We went into the house, a very large long, low bungalow with creepers and grape vines growing all over and round it, providing some welcome shade. We were shown into our bedroom, a small room with two beds, a small chest of drawers with a washing bowl and jug on the top and a small tallboy, or wardrobe, in it. The farmer brought our luggage in, and with the big sea chest and two cases in there, there wasn't much room to move around. He told us that dinner would be ready in half an hour, leaving us to unpack. As the door closed, Mum sat down on one of the beds, and I saw big tears coursing silently down her face. Not being used to too much affection between us, I cuddled her clumsily, and she enfolded me in her arms – we grew closer in those few minutes than we had ever been before. She said nothing and quickly regained her composure. We unpacked a few things, and then went through to the dining room, welcomed by the delicious smell of a beef stew. We had not eaten since breakfast, and the farmer's wife was a good cook. She opened the refrigerator to get some milk out for us children to drink and my mouth dropped open at the sight of the food in there – eggs, butter, cheese, bacon, milk, and lamb chops – all the things that were on ration in England in tiny portions each week. It seemed to me that there was enough food in there to feed a whole town, let alone just one family. There was an awkward silence as we sat down to eat, but the conversation was started by the farmer telling Mum that when she gathered the wood in the morning, she must watch out for spiders, snakes and goannas. The two older boys took great delight in elaborating on their Father's instructions, warning us about tiny red-backed spiders who lurk behind toilet seats and bite your bottom, their bites often being lethal; and big trapdoor spiders that jump out of little holes in the ground with a trapdoor on the top to catch their prey, also with a poisonous bite. They told us about the black and brown snakes whose bites are also highly venomous. I asked what a 'goanna' was, and was told that it was a big lizard that climbed up into trees, and would jump on you and bite you. The bite would develop into a rash, and every year on the anniversary of the bite, you would get a painful rash come up. It made me feel very vulnerable – I hadn't expected problems like this … why didn't they tell us in Australia House so that we would have at least been forewarned? The only spiders that I had ever come across were little spindly daddy-long-legs that you found on old walls in England (and I have to confess with great shame that I even used to pull their legs off without a conscience). So began my lifelong hysterical, illogical terror of all eight-legged creatures, and I still I have problems in dealing with them today.

After dessert, Mum asked if it would be OK if we went to bed, as it had been a long day. After saying a polite goodnight to the family, we went into the bedroom and completed the unpacking of our cases and climbed gratefully into our beds. I was soon asleep, but Mum told me years later that she had cried all night long, so lacking in confidence was she at being able to perform her arduous duties properly. She was, however, determined to do her best and prove that she was capable of the task ahead of her.

We got up at 5.30am the next morning, washed, dressed, and went into the kitchen. The farmer was there, and he showed us where the wheelbarrow and axe was, and pointed us to the area where we would find the wood. We were amazed at how cold the morning was, our breath condensing on the cool air. Mum said she was glad she had brought all our woollens with us; we were certainly going to need them. Ever mindful of spiders, snakes and goannas, Mum started to wield the axe, but she had been a smoker since her teens and was soon out of breath. I took over the task of chopping the logs up ... fortunately the wood was rotten and dry and we soon had the wheelbarrow full. Back at the house, The farmer showed Mum how to clean out the ashes and light the fire, and the hotplates were soon hot enough for Mum to prepare scrambled egg on toast for seven of us, and cereal for the baby. The two older boys collected their satchels and went to the front gate to wait for the school bus to take them into Corowa. The farmer told Mum that he would take us into Corowa the following afternoon to enrol me at Corowa Primary School. After breakfast we washed up, I wiped up and had to ask the farmer's wife where everything belonged, and she seemed impatient with the fact that I didn't know … but then, how could I? Mum's next task was to dust and sweep the house and the farmer's wife, carrying the baby with her, followed us around watching every move we made. Perhaps she thought we were untrustworthy and might steal something, but it felt odd to be so watched. I noticed what very pale blue eyes she had, and then I noticed something else that made me smile – her hair was on crooked! When Mum and I got a minute in the bedroom on our own, I mentioned it, and was warned on pain of death not to say anything about it to anyone, but more particularly, not to smile or laugh if the wig was on crooked again as the farmer's wife didn't miss a thing.

By the time we completed the cleaning chores the farmer had returned from his work on the farm. Mum cooked lamb chops and mashed potatoes for lunch and in the afternoon she did a load of ironing that was piling up in the laundry. The time passed quickly as I sat beside her, chattering about our trip out from England. The boys came in from school and settled down to do their homework. That evening Mum cooked eggs and baked beans with cold ham for tea, which seemed to go down well with the family, and we had fruit for dessert, so no real culinary challenges for her there. We cleared up after tea whilst the family went into the lounge to play board games, and then we excused ourselves for an early night – Mum was utterly exhausted and we both fell asleep quickly, sleeping soundly.

The next morning we were up early again, collected the wood and got the fire going in the range. We had cereal for breakfast, and the two boys left for school. During the morning Mum and I cleaned all the windows – they all had fly-screens which had to be removed before we could actually clean them, so it took us a long time. When they were done, the farmer's wife inspected them and made us do some again that she was not satisfied with.

At lunchtime the farmer returned, and we had ham sandwiches for lunch. He told us to get in the car and we headed the ten miles into Corowa. I was impatient to see what the town was like, as it seemed odd to be living right out in the country after the busy bustle of a London suburb. Mum commented on the fact that we passed a small airport, and the farmer told us that it was used mainly for freight, but that there were a few domestic flights in and out of there and also quite a few private planes operated from there. He said that aircraft were very important in Australia because of the great distances between homesteads. For instance, there was a Flying Doctor Service that operated in the remote areas, and also flights that delivered and collected school work from farms where the children lived too far away from a school to attend, and did their lessons by listening to radio broadcasts. I was fascinated by all of this, and half-wished that I could be one of those children. By this time we were in Corowa, a town of about 3,000 people with a hospital, a junior and a senior school, a cinema, an Anglican Church and a Roman Catholic Church, a showground ... and ten, yes ten, pubs! Mum was not very impressed with this fact, as drinking was not on her list of priorities. The farmer took us on a brief tour of the town, pointing out the main features. The houses were very typical, and most of the side streets were surfaced with dirt and gravel, but the main roads were surfaced with tarmac – Sanger Street (the main street), Honour Avenue which changed into the Albury Road and led to Albury and the Riverina Highway, Bow Street which changed into the Redlands Road and went to the airport, and the Deniliquin Road which went to Mulwala and Deniliquin. Sanger Street ran uphill from the direction of the Murray River, a broad river with a long bridge which crossed it to Wahgunyah in Victoria. Sanger Street was a broad street lined each side with shops, there was a post office, and of course, the pubs, all ten of them dotted on either side of the street. The balconies above some of the shops had beautiful lace-work wrought iron railings around them, and I thought it was one of the prettiest streets I had ever seen. The farmer then headed for Corowa Primary School – my first experience of an Australian Education.

Chapter 12 – School

We pulled up outside the school, and the farmer said he would pick us up at the same place in an hour. The school was built of the same weatherboarding with a corrugated iron roof as were most of the houses, had a smaller building opposite the main one, and a long playground segregated into girls' and boys' areas by a wire fence, with a sandy surface. At one end of the smaller of the two buildings there was a large area which had a construction with open sides and a corrugated iron roof, a sort of shelter from the sun, I presumed. As we walked up the school steps to the big wooden porch, a lady emerged and asked us what we wanted. We learned later that she was Mrs Bryan, the wife of the Headmaster of the High School, and she taught sewing at the Primary School once a week. She was ginger-haired, and I was soon to learn that she had a fiery temper to match her hair. Mum told her that we were newly-arrived in Australia and that she wanted to enrol me at the school. The lady disappeared into the school, and was eventually followed out by a tall, grey-haired man with glasses. He introduced himself as Mr Deasey, the Headmaster, and he asked me what subjects I had learned at school in England. I was a bit tongue-tied, so with a gesture of impatience, he fired times tables questions at me. I'm sure I got them all wrong, mainly because I hadn't had any schooling for over a month, and I was a bit rusty on my answers. He told Mum that I could start the following day, a Friday – I think Mum was hoping that he would say start the following Monday so that I could help her with the chores, but she was glad that at last I was back into education. Then he ran through the times of school and school uniform rules, and returned back into the building. We were astounded that he hadn't even asked us inside to show us around, but that was that – we were 'dismissed'. As we still had three quarters of an hour before we were due to be collected we wandered up the nearest street and it brought us to the Monument, a quite impressive cenotaph surrounded by lawns. Opposite that were the Corowa, and Coreen Shire, Council Offices. Coreen Shire was the name of the area surrounding Corowa town, consisting mostly of large sheep farms like the one we were staying at. Honour Avenue, the road to Albury, started near the Monument; it was a broad avenue lined with kurrajong trees, their creamy blossoms contrasting with the intensity of the blue sky, and with mainly residences on either side. From here we walked to the top of Sanger Street, and saw the Rex Cinema, some Gardens called the Victoria Gardens, and a big furniture shop called Maples.

It was time to go back to the school to be collected, and we had only been there a few minutes when the farmer arrived, so we climbed into the car. He didn't ask how we had got on; I suppose he assumed that I would have to be taken into the school anyway and the journey home was completed largely in silence. When we arrived at the farm, the farmer's wife had obviously been sitting reading all afternoon, and she immediately ordered Mum to start preparing tea, so Mum and I set about preparing cheese and tomato sandwiches. The farmer's wife said this was not enough, as the boys only take sandwiches to school for their mid-day meal, so she told Mum to make some chips to go with them. Mum had never made chips, she had always bought them from a fish and chip shop, so the farmer's wife impatiently gave her the directions on how to do it – chip pan on the hotplate, peel and cut the potatoes and put them in the pan. Unfortunately she forgot to tell Mum to dry the chips on a towel, so when the fat was hot enough and Mum tipped the chips into the pan, the water and fat together boiled up and all over the hotplate. As Mum cleaned up the mess as best she could, it was obvious that the family were angry.

During the meal the boys chattered away about their day at school and told me that they had seen us talking to 'Greasy Deasey' out of the classroom window. I told them that I was going to travel in with them on the bus tomorrow, and that we would be unpacking our sea chest after dinner to get my gym slip and blouses out ready for school. We cleared away after we had eaten and Mum and I went into our bedroom to tackle unpacking the chest. There were books in there that would probably have to remain in the chest, as we had nowhere to put them, but we would need those warm clothes. The autumn climate (of course, the climates are completely reversed in Australia, which seemed strange to us) during each day reflected all four seasons – freezing cold winter temperatures early in the morning; spring-like weather through the morning, warming up to very hot sunshine during the afternoon, then back through autumn temperatures in the early evening into the coldness of a winter day later in the evening. We had almost forgotten exactly what was in the chest, as the last time we had seen it was when Pickford's collected it from Camelot Street to transport it to the ship for us over a month ago. Mum found the key for the big padlock on the front and carefully raised the lid. What we saw next filled us both with horror. Our clothes were a heaving mass of maggots – apparently Mum had managed to pack a couple of pregnant moths in with the woollens and these had made a wonderful breeding ground during the month at sea. I felt quite sick at the stench and Mum shut the lid quickly. She went through and asked the farmer what she should do – he took one look at the smelly contents of the chest and angrily hauled it outside. He was about to pour paraffin into the chest and set light to it when Mum begged him to let her remove her books, which, although covered in the squirming mass, were undamaged. He let her do this, so we brushed off all the books and photograph albums, and then we stood back and watched as what was left of our warm clothing went up in smoke, including my gym slip and blouses. Mum promised to get me a new school uniform as soon as she had been paid her first week's wages. The chest was left outside to cool down and we made our way back into our room, where the big silent tears started to fall again, and this time a cuddle was all we could do to console each other.

The next day we were up at 5.30am again, got the wood in for the stove, cleaned the top of the stove properly where the fat had boiled over, cleaned out yesterday's ashes and lit the fire. When the stove was ready, Mum prepared a breakfast of poached eggs on toast (Mum's repertoire was quite limited when it came to cooking!) and I made three packed lunches and prepared for my first day at my new school. Mum let me wear my best dress and cardigan, but I dreaded another telling-off for not being in uniform like the one I had received at Camelot Street School for the same reason. The boys and I walked to the gate and waited for the school bus to arrive. They jumped on before me and went to the back of the bus with their friends, so I sat on my own in one of the front seats. I gradually became aware that something kept stinging the back of my neck and, on turning round, saw that the boys at the back had elastic bands and were firing folded up pieces of paper at me. I was so miserable, feeling that I did not have a friend in the world, and when more children boarded the bus at various stops along the route I sunk further and further into fear and despair. At each stop the two boys shouted out to the newcomers on board "*She's the bloody pommy kid we have staying with us*", and "*the maggots ate all her clothes!*". Although I didn't understand what a 'pommy' was, the language shocked me as it was the first time I had heard this expression and bad language from anyone, let alone children (I never heard my Mum swear once during her lifetime), but I was more shocked at the attitude of the children. Some of them spat at me as they passed my seat, some pulled the bunches in my hair until it hurt and others joined in the onslaught of missiles fired from elastic bands from the back of the bus. The driver remained impassive throughout this torment, and this time it was my turn for the big silent tears to well up, but I was determined not to let them see me crying. It was with great relief that we arrived at the school and I was able to disembark. I ran into the playground where the other students were gathering, but the farmer's sons were relentless in their tormenting, and by the time the whistle was blown for Assembly I was well known as 'that bloody pommy kid'.

Assembly was held between the two buildings, and consisted of the singing of a song called 'Advance, Australia Fair', and the holding up of a handkerchief by each child. I did not know that we had to have a handkerchief, so on that first morning I was hauled up in front of the whole school and asked where my handkerchief was. When I began to cry and say that I didn't realise that I needed one, there broke out a concerted derisory laugh from all the children. I resolved from that moment on to always carry a handkerchief in future. Thankfully, nothing was said about my not wearing uniform, so I guess everyone knew that it would take a while to equip me properly for school. I was fascinated by the fact that some of the children were bare-footed ... nobody paid any attention to this, it was obviously quite common. I was glad I had my sturdy school shoes on, as the gravel looked quite sharp and uncomfortable to walk on, but the shoeless children didn't seem to notice. It seems strange looking back to think that my not having a handkerchief should attract such ridicule, but not having shoes on was accepted without a murmur!

It is worthy of note here that the words of 'Advance, Australia Fair' have changed since I was a child.[2]

We filed into our classrooms, with me following the two boys, which fortunately turned out to be the right thing to do. Our Form Teacher was Mr Deasey, the Headmaster, and as he called the register I was relieved to hear my name called. At least I was in the right class. What I didn't realise was that I had been put in the bottom group for my year, together with the farmer's boys, probably because of my poor performance when Mr Deasey had asked me the times tables questions the day before.

The entire school day passed in a mixture of confusion and fear. At playtime and lunch-time I kept myself separate from everyone, eating my packed lunch in the shelter attached to the small building and watching the girls playing a ball game which I would love to have joined in, but daren't ask. The cross-boards on the roof trusses formed a bar about ten inches wide, and a girl

[2] Then, we sang a version of the second verse as follows:

"When gallant Cook of Albion came, To trace wide oceans o'er,
True British courage bore him on 'til he landed on our shore,
And there he raised old England's flag, The standard of the brave –
With all her faults we love her still Britannia rules the waves.
In joyful strains then let us sing, Advance Australia fair!"

The change is less than subtle, and now the first verse of the Anthem is as follows:

Australians all let us rejoice, For we are young and free;
We've golden soil and wealth for toil, Our home is girt by sea;
Our land abounds in Nature's gifts Of beauty rich and rare;
In history's page, let every stage Advance Australia fair!
In joyful strains then let us sing, "Advance Australia fair!"
© *Commonwealth of Australia*

The modern Anthem incorporates some of the verse that we sang in the 1950's, but the change is noticeable. 'Gallant Cook of Albion fame' has been relegated to the back benches! The new version was adopted after a referendum in 1984, which rejected 'Waltzing Matilda' and the British National Anthem in favour of a two-verse modified version of 'Advance, Australia Fair' to become the formal National Anthem of Australia.

stood either side of the bar, one throwing a ball at the bar and catching it as it bounced back until the ball missed the bar, or hit it at an angle and bounced onto the floor, whereupon it became the turn of the girl opposite to see how many times she could hit the bar in succession. I watched the game, fascinated, counting the successful hits. In the afternoon the boys and the girls played sports, segregated in the playground by the wire fence that ran almost to the bottom of the playground. The boys played cricket and the girls played a version of cricket played with a paddle-shaped bat, designed especially for girls and called Vigaro. I had never played this before, and no-one wanted me in their team so I sat under a tree and watched. At the end of the afternoon I was relieved to be getting onto the school bus for the ride home. However, the torment continued until we arrived back at the farm and I couldn't wait to get Mum alone and tell her how dreadful it had been. When I told her what the children had called me, she too found it difficult to understand what it meant – she was very angry and wanted to tell the parents how badly behaved their boys had been, but politeness dictated that she said nothing ... she told me that we were guests in their home and we shouldn't complain. She had had a bad day, being criticised by the farmer's wife for almost everything she did and having to do some of the cleaning chores twice to satisfy this strange lady. She had been told that the next day she would have to do the washing and she had been shown how to work the washing machine, but never having seen one before, she was nervous and didn't want to make a mess of it. The following day being Saturday, at least I was going to be there to help her hang the washing out.

The farmer's wife had a huge joint of cooked beef in the refrigerator, so we had a cold beef salad for tea – this was relatively easy to prepare, so Mum didn't have a problem with that. She had made a batch of buns that afternoon and served these as a dessert. Not being a good cook, according to the boys, the buns tasted 'salty' so they were left half-eaten. Poor Mum, she tried so hard. After tea we set to and went outside and cleaned out the sea chest of all the charred remains of our woollens – being made of sturdy metal it had survived the fire very well, and after a good scrub with hot soapy water it was ready to be used again. We took it indoors, and Mum replaced all her treasured photograph albums and books in it. It had been a stressful day for both of us so we went to bed early. This time we slept in the same bed, cuddled up close, needing so much to feel support from each other. The feeling that Australia was Utopia was rapidly disappearing – it was beginning to be a nightmare for both of us. I'm glad we didn't know at this point just how much worse it was going to get …

The next morning we were up early again, fetched the wood, and got the fire in the stove going. We had devised a routine together, and we were pleased that at least this part of the day went according to plan. We put a huge pan on the stove to heat it for the washing machine and after a breakfast of eggs and bacon, we collected all the dirty washing we could find. The boys' dirty washing was easy to find … it was scattered all around their bedroom floors. We had put our few bits in the bottom of our tallboy, so we put those in the laundry separately, and the farmer's wife brought the rest, including a bucket of soiled terry-towelling nappies that the baby had used.

She told Mum to wash those by hand before they went into the washing machine as the last load, after all the other things were done. Mum had never used a washing machine before, but between us we managed to sort the clothes into piles, keeping ours separate from theirs, got the hot water into the machine and the first load in under the ever-watchful eye of the farmer's wife. Her wig was on crooked again, but there was no flicker of amusement on our faces, so frightened were we of what might happen if she saw us laughing at her. When the first load was finished we put another load in and took the first load out into the garden, where there was a huge 'whirligig' linen line. We had never seen anything like this before, but what a great idea – instead of having a huge long linen line stretched across the garden as they did in England, this had more hanging space in a compact area, looking for all the world like a giant spider's web on a pole. The whole line revolved in the wind, and with the autumn sun beating down, the clothes dried very quickly. We managed to get most of the loads done, by which time the water was getting quite dirty. Mums asked should she put another pan on the stove and heat some more water up, but the farmer's wife said no, there were only our clothes and the nappies still to be done, so the water in the machine would suffice.

At this point it was nearing the time for the midday meal, so the farmer's wife stopped us doing the washing, saying we could finish it after lunch. We peeled potatoes and prepared vegetables, and the farmer came in from the farm. When the meal of cold roast beef and vegetables was ready all eight of us sat down to eat, the baby in his high chair near his mother. At first there was the usual uncomfortable silence, but then the farmer surprised us by saying that he had decided to move us out of the house into the shearer's quarters, where we would have more room to spread out a bit. He asked us to pack all our things up after lunch and he said he would load them into the car to move them, as the shearer's accommodation was situated quite some way from the house. I had seen the buildings from a distance and they looked similar to most of the other farm buildings – long, low sheds with tin roofs. I felt quite relieved at this news – we would be away from the constant surveillance of his wife, and have more space. I timidly asked if there were spiders in the shearer's rooms and the boys managed to scare me half to death with their stories about just how big the spiders were out there! By this time I had developed quite a phobia about spiders, but the farmer told me not to worry, they wouldn't bother me.

After lunch, the farmer's wife told us to get the washing in and then pack our things. We didn't really have a lot to pack, as the books were already in the chest, so we collected our still-unwashed clothes from the laundry and packed them into our cases. Mum stripped the beds and put the sheets in the laundry and the farmer came and put all our possessions in the back of the estate car, and told us to get in. Once we were in the car, he told Mum that it was General Election Day in Australia and that he had registered her as a voter, which he actually had been obliged to do as voting in a General Election in Australia was mandatory in those days – he was taking us in to Corowa so that Mum could vote. This sounded perfectly reasonable to us, especially as he added that there was a big fine if you didn't vote. When we got into Corowa he parked outside the hall with a big sign outside saying 'Polling Station', pointed to the hall and told Mum to go inside to vote – he even told her who to vote for, as she had no knowledge of Australian politics. She got out of the car taking her handbag with her and as soon as she disappeared out of sight, he told me to get out of the car, too. He quickly unloaded the boot of our belongings, turned to me and said "*Tell your Mother she's not suitable*" – and then he drove off at full speed. I was stunned, and watched his car disappearing in a cloud of dust. Mum came out of the hall, saw the luggage on the verge and asked me what had happened. I told her that the farmer had told me to get out of the car and what he had said, and I am thankful to this day that I had no idea at that moment of the enormity of our desperate situation – we had been in Australia a little less than a week, 12,500 miles away from the place we knew as home, we had no money, Mum had no job, we knew no-one, we had nowhere to go, and Peter was over 50 miles away and apart from writing a letter, impossible to contact.

Chapter 13 – Abandoned

Mum slumped down onto the chest and the silent tears started again. Being Mum, she of indomitable spirit, she did not allow her self-pity to last for long, so she decided to go to the Post Office to see if there was any accommodation available nearby. We balanced the two cases on the chest and carried it between us to Sanger Street, only to find that the Post Office was closed, it being a Saturday; and all the other offices and shops were closed because of the General Election. There was nothing else for it but to ask in a pub if they had any accommodation, which Mum found wholly distasteful. Mum's Lancashire accent was very pronounced and in the first pub we went into she barely had time to get out the fact that she wanted accommodation before the landlord said "*Not so likely, you're a bloody pommy, and we don't want those in here!*". Shocked, Mum now understood the implications of being a 'bloody pommy'. We trudged down Sanger Street, struggling to manage the chest and the cases between us, so Mum told me to wait under one of the trees in the shade with the luggage, whilst she proceeded to call at the other pubs that offered accommodation – the Australia, the Corowa, the Newmarket, the Globe, the Star and most of the others. Astonishingly, she got the same reaction in all of them. She came back up the street to where I was, and said "*Come on, there is one more pub left, let's try that one*". We made our way down to the Terminus Hotel, right down at the bottom end of the street, and went in. The landlord's wife came out from a back room, and Mum asked if they had a room vacant. The lady told us there wasn't, not for 'pommies'. Mum, by this time at the end of her tether, burst into tears and explained what had happened to us, carefully avoiding saying which farm we had come from. The landlady took pity on us and said we could sleep in the back lounge on the settee, but that we had to be out before 6am the next morning as, if her customers found out that she was giving us shelter, she would lose them to other pubs. We gratefully followed her through to the lounge with our luggage, she told us where the toilet was and told us to stay in the room and be quiet. We were by this time so worn out and emotionally drained that we made ourselves comfortable and I fell asleep in Mum's arms. Poor Mum – here she was at 51 with a child of ten, in a strange country and not knowing what on earth would happen to us in the coming days. It must have been dreadful for her, but her fighting spirit was to stand her in good stead over the next few weeks and, despite not being suitable as a domestic help, she possessed other qualities that would enable her to prove that she was not yet beaten.

The next morning the landlady came in at 5.30am with a cup of tea for each of us and asked Mum to leave by 6am. Mum told her that as soon as she had some money she would come back and pay her for her kindness, but the landlady said she would prefer it if we didn't come near the place again. What sort of country was this to be so prejudiced against a woman and her child? Mum then enquired if there were any Bed and Breakfast places that we could try, but the landlady said it would be unlikely that any of them would take us in. As an afterthought she added *"You could try Mrs Hornsey. She might be desperate enough to take you in"*. Mum was given Mrs Hornsey's address, 24 Walker Street, and we were told where to find it. It was not close by, but she said it was within walking distance. Relieved at the possibility of somewhere to stay we put the cases on top of the chest, took a handle each, and quietly left the hotel. We had seen some pretty Gardens when we briefly explored Corowa two days previously, the Victoria Gardens, so we made our way up there and sat until about 8.30am. Then we trundled our way up to Walker Street. Number 24 was a typical single-storey house with a corrugated iron roof, surrounded by a large garden and with a separate small garage on the right-hand side, set well back from the road down a grass drive. We went up to the front door and knocked. A lady came from around the back accompanied by a black Cocker Spaniel, and asked us what we wanted. We must have looked a strange sight, stood there with our luggage. When Mum explained that we had been given her name as someone who might be able to offer us accommodation, she started to say no, then stopped and thought for a minute. She then said *"Well, my husband has recently left me with five kids to bring up, so I can't have you in the house, but he has taken the car, and the garage is empty – you can rent that if you want*". Mum was astounded, but she knew by this time that she was unlikely to get anywhere else, so she asked to look at the garage. Mrs Hornsey took us down the garden and through the side door into what was basically a weatherboard shed about 15ft by 10ft, with a corrugated iron roof, a small window on the front wall, a concrete floor, and two large wooden doors at one end where the garage opened out onto the grass driveway. My Mum, bless her, the least domesticated lady in the whole world, obviously felt that she could make a home out of this place, so she agreed to rent it. She told Mrs Hornsey that we had no money, but that she was going to get a job and would pay rent as soon as she had received her first wages. Mrs Hornsey reluctantly agreed to this, which looking back, seems amazing. There must have been something about Mum that led her to believe that she would be trustworthy. It hadn't occurred to Mum that the very reason that had led to the refusals in the pubs to accommodate us (her Lancashire accent giving away the fact that we were English) might also prevent her getting a job. She had good secretarial skills and by hook or by crook she was going to find work! Mrs Hornsey told us to wait and as soon as she was out of sight I reminded Mum that I still had the ten shillings that I had won in the Deck Quoits competition on the boat – I said that she could have that for the rent. Mum took it, quietly said that she would use it for food not rent, and repay me as soon as she could. Mrs Hornsey returned to her house and shortly after that her two eldest children, Vincent and Tessie carried a single fold-up bed into the garage, with some bed linen, a kettle, a primus stove, a bowl, a bucket with a lid to use as a toilet, some crockery, cutlery, a saucepan, a teapot and a packet of tea, and finally a small card table and two wooden chairs. Vincent showed us where the tap was in the garden and the 'dunny' at the back of the house where we could empty the toilet bucket and then they left us on our own in our new home. We made up the bed and Mum sat down on it, grinned at me and said "At least we didn't have to wash those nappies!". From that moment on I knew that we were going to be alright.

Chapter 14 – Settling In

Mum borrowed a broom and duster from Mrs Hornsey and we set about cleaning the garage to make it habitable. There were grease and oil stains on the floor and a couple of shelves with tins of paint on them, but by the time we had finished it began to look presentable. She knew that there would be many things that we would need, but they would have to come later. We were intrigued by the sound of horses close by, accompanied by a lot of swearing and the cracking of a whip. We learned later that a man called Jack Hall lived next door and his back yard had been converted into a corral where he broke in horses. The unavoidable outcome of this was that we were inundated with flies and had to keep the door shut most of the time to stop the garage being invaded by them! Many times I sat on the fence and watched the swearing, sweating man breaking the spirit of these lovely creatures. He would tether their front feet together and use the whip freely, finally getting them to be compliant, more from fear than choice, I think.

Mrs Hornsey came down mid-morning to see if we were alright. She stayed a while, telling us briefly that she had asthma really badly and was unable to work. She told us that there was a dairy round the corner which was always open, where we could buy milk and eggs, so we made our way round there and discovered that you needed a billy-can to buy milk. The lady in the dairy said they sold them in the town, so we could only buy some eggs. She had some billy-cans hanging on hooks in the dairy, and although she didn't say anything, we felt that she might have been a little more helpful if we had been Australian! Looking back I think it was really sad that we had begun to expect discrimination so early, but having already suffered a lot of it, I suppose it was inevitable. When we got back I filled the kettle from the tap in the garden, and made a pot of tea. We boiled some water in the saucepan and poached a couple of eggs each, drank our tea without milk and sugar and then set about washing the dirty clothes that were still packed in our cases. Mum borrowed a big tin bath from Mrs Hornsey and we boiled a couple of kettles and set to with soap and hot water, hand washing everything. There was an old 'whirlygig' line in the garden and the clothes were soon hung out and drying rapidly in the sunshine. It was lovely to have fresh clothes in our cases again. For tea we had scrambled eggs and another cup of milkless tea, and decided to have an early night.

The next morning I washed and dressed ready for school and Mum prepared herself to go job-hunting. As I left the garage Vincent, Tessie, Shirley and Lenny were also just leaving, so they said I could walk to school with them. I was so relieved not to be facing the bus ride into school from the farm ... I don't think I could have coped with that treatment again. We passed the Flour mill with the two big wheat silos, and came to the main road, where we separated from Vincent as he was going to the High School. I felt safer arriving at school with the Hornsey children, but they quickly joined their friends and left me on my own. The bell rang and we lined up for Assembly ... and this time I had a freshly-laundered handkerchief pinned to my dress. The day passed uneventfully, but I was still ostracised and isolated. Never mind, I was getting back into the swing of school, and enjoyed the lessons. In the afternoon we had English, and I was told that I would have to give a 'lecturette', a three-minute talk on any subject I liked, and I had a week to prepare it. It would be given standing at the front of the class, there would be ten minutes for questions, and then I would be given a mark out of ten for it. This filled me with terror, as I had never stood in front of a class apart from showing my postcard that Peter had sent me from Ceylon, where the teacher had done most of the talking. Three other children were also advised that they had to give their 'lecturette' the following week. As we left school I heard them expressing the same fears as I was feeling, so that made me feel a little better. I looked for the Hornsey children but they had already left, so I started for Walker Street, hoping I could find my way back without getting lost. I was surprised to feel a tap on my shoulder, and two boys drew alongside me and said "*Hey, you're that English girl, aren't you?*". I heard their Australian accents and thought that they might be going to torment me like the boys on the bus, but one of them said "*We're English too*". Then they ran ahead, and I saw them disappear into a house further on. I couldn't wait to get back to the garage and tell Mum what they had said.

Earlier that day, Mum had started at the top end of Sanger Street, calling at every shop and business on both sides of the street. There was a bakery, dress shop, garage, Maples the big furniture store that we had seen two days previously when the farmer had brought us to the school, a dentist, a bank, cafés, and other establishments, but the answer was the same in every one – "*Sorry, we have no vacancy to fill*" … and some of them even said "*We don't give bloody pommies work round here*". I think Mum started to believe that she would never get a job, when she spied the office of a firm of solicitors, John Strong & Co, just down a side street. Fortunately the office needed another secretary, and as Mum had worked at the Law Courts in London her experience stood her in good stead. She passed her secretarial tests with flying colours as the typewriter was an older model of the one she had been used to using at the Law Courts. When I arrived home Mum was beaming all over her face and she told me the good news straight away. This turn of events was so bizarre that we were both stunned. On Saturday we were 'dumped' by an uncaring, hard man, and today (Monday) we had accommodation (of sorts!), and Mum had a job.

Through her work, Mum was introduced to another solicitor in the town, Mr Lethbridge, and she overheard him mention that he needed a babysitter that night. Mr Lethbridge had a young family, two daughters and a son, and when Mum offered her services as a babysitter he was really grateful. Apparently they had been let down by their babysitter who had to leave Corowa suddenly because of a family emergency and he was desperate, as he and his wife were due to go to an important dinner party that evening. Mum explained that she had a daughter, but he said that would be fine, I could go along too.

Mum had convinced herself that Mr Lethbridge must be trustworthy as he was obviously a respected member of the local community. He had arranged to pick us up at Walker Street at 6pm and true to his word he turned up in a gleaming Holden car on the dot. We stood waiting at the gate, as Mum was too embarrassed to let him know that we lived in the garage. Mum introduced me to him, and I liked him straight away. He had a lovely crinkly smile and he looked very handsome in his tuxedo. He drove us to his house on the outskirts of Corowa, a lovely single-storey place set in a big garden. He introduced us to his wife, a gracious, beautiful lady, and his three children, two pretty girls and a little golden-haired boy, Philip, who we were told to call Phippa. I didn't understand why I hadn't seen the girls at school until they told us that they attended the Roman Catholic School. We were shown over the house and told to help ourselves to anything we needed from the fridge. The children had already had their tea, so all Mum had to do was read them a story, make sure that they washed and cleaned their teeth and put them to bed. This she did, and we never heard a sound from the children for the rest of the evening. We ate a modest salad supper from the fridge, marvelling yet again at how much food it contained. The Lethbridges arrived home at about midnight, checked the children who were all soundly asleep, and then Mr Lethbridge paid Mum in cash before he took us back to Walker Street. We slid carefully into bed (it was a bit rickety with two people in it!) and I think Mum slept soundly for the first time in a week. This was the start of a four-year long babysitting commitment with the Lethbridges, one of the nicest families you could wish to meet.

Early next morning Mum went up to see Mrs Hornsey to pay her some rent. She wanted ten shillings a week for the garage, so Mum gave her the money and mentioned that she needed to buy me a gym slip and some blouses. Mrs Hornsey told Mum immediately that she was fond of dressmaking, she had some suitable material so, if Mum wanted her to, she would make me a couple of gym slips. All she needed to do was measure me, she could do at least one of them that day and the two would be five shillings. I went up to the house and was measured straight away.

When I went back to the garage I suddenly remembered about the two English boys and I told Mum my news. She was intrigued as she didn't realise that there were any other English people in town. She asked me to ask the boys what their surname was. We both had a wash, had breakfast and then we got ready, Mum looking really smart for her first day in the office. I walked to school with the Hornseys and I felt more confident during the day, as I did well at my lessons, although I was still being left alone by the children. I tried to find out the names of the English boys, but as girls and boys were segregated at playtime and lunchtime I was not able to speak to them. The Hornseys had left by the time I got out of school, so I waited to see if I could see the boys again, but I must have missed them so I walked slowly home. I read until Mum got home – she had been shopping at lunchtime and had bought food, so we had a stew for tea and fruit for dessert. It was the first proper meal we had eaten for 3 days ... we even had milk and sugar in our tea. Mum told me that she was horrified at having to pay one penny each for Oxo cubes – they were 6 for a penny in London! Other food items were comparatively expensive, except meat, which was not only cheaper, but certainly more plentiful, considering that we had been rationed to two ounces per person per week in England.

Mrs Hornsey brought down the gym slip she had made which fitted perfectly, so Mum paid her for that and promised to get me some blouses as soon as she had some more money at the end of the week.

Mum had had a good day in the office, and made the comment that she was surprised to note that most of the things she used in the work she did – typewriter, eraser, ink, pencils, pens etc – were all 'Made in England'. I think that really cheered her up. After tea we washed up, and when I told her that I had been unable to speak to the two boys she suggested that I show her the house that they had disappeared into, so we walked to the house and knocked on the door. A lady answered and Mum explained that we had just moved into Corowa and had heard that there were some other English people there, so she thought it might be nice to make contact with them. The lady seemed pleased to see us and invited us in. Their surname was Clark – she introduced her husband and her two sons, Brian and Robert. She also had a cute little girl of about 2 years old. She made us welcome, giving us tea and biscuits, but after hearing about our experiences, she explained that they had been in Corowa for a few months, and had received the same sort of treatment that we had experienced from the locals. She told us that they were moving away from Corowa shortly as lots of people had told them to get out of Corowa and go to one of the big cities where they wouldn't stand out so much. Her husband had been unable to obtain much work, and when Mum explained about the job she had found in the solicitor's office, Mrs Clark said she was very lucky to find someone who was prepared to employ her. It was disappointing to find that they would be moving away soon, just when we had got to know them, but it sort of made us feel a bit better that we were not being 'got at' because of who we were, merely because of the fact that we were English. Mrs Clark asked Mum if she wanted to buy one of the boys' bicycles – a battered, rusty old fixed-wheel one (where the pedals have to turn continuously) – for two shillings. Mum thought this was a bargain, so she paid for it and I wheeled it home. We gave the Clarks our address and asked them to keep in touch, but we never heard from them after they moved away.

When we got the bike home we realised that it needed a lot of attention and was not useable until it was repaired. I found some bright emerald green paint on the shelf in the garage, and set about painting the bike frame. I was pretty pleased with the result, at least it **looked** better than it did! Vincent came down the garden to see what I was doing and he volunteered to repair the bike for me. I was so grateful – he oiled everything, tightened the chain, and put a new pedal on for me. He checked the brakes and, as the tyres were OK, it was ready to ride. There was only one problem … I had never owned a bicycle before and had no idea how to ride one. Mum said she would teach me at the weekend, so I had to be patient.

The rest of the week seemed to go quite quickly, and I was really enjoying school. Although I didn't realise it at the time, the British education system was a year ahead of the Australian one, so in effect, I was academically a year more advanced than they were. As I settled down to school work, I had no idea that coming first in most subjects was going to mean a whole lot of trouble for the future. I began to feel completely cut off from the other children, who were still tormenting me because I didn't have a proper school uniform, because I didn't have a handkerchief on the first day, and because I was, well ... just English, a 'bloody pommy' that they would rather do without. Mr Deasey was a bit offhand, but he did usually mark my work fairly and try to include me in all the activities. He changed me from the group that I had originally been put into to one of a higher standard. I was grateful for this as it took me away from the vicinity of the farmer's sons, who had not spoken one word to me since Mum and I were dumped in Corowa so disgracefully by their Dad. It also didn't go down too well with the children in the group I joined so they ignored me completely.

On one occasion Mr Deasey asked me to stand up and read a chapter from a book called 'Australian Legends' about a dog who had been faithful to his bullock train driver master, even when his master had died, remaining sat on his master's tucker box until he died himself. There was a memorial to the dog just north of a town called Gundagai. To me, the pronunciation of this place-name should be 'Gun-daggy', which is what I read out. I was immediately faced with howls of laughter and derision from all the children and Mr Deasey, and taunts of 'stupid', 'dil' and 'idiot' rang in my ears. I was told by Mr Deasey that the pronunciation was 'Gun-da-guy', but I was so flustered I was unable to continue. This got me zero marks for reading, which I felt was totally unfair. From then on I often had 'Gun-daggy' shouted at me in the playground and even in the town away from school, too. It stuck in my mind so vividly; to this day I cannot read that place name without pronouncing it 'Gun-daggy'!

On a Thursday afternoon, the girls in our class had Sewing and the boys did Woodwork. Mrs Bryan, the lady I had seen on the day we visited the school to enrol me, was a striking woman with red hair and a sour face. She told me that I had to bring some money to school the following week to buy some fabric from her, as the class was making aprons and I would have to catch up with them. There was only one sewing machine, so nobody progressed very fast, and most of the sewing had to be done by hand. Mrs Bryan was very strict, we were not allowed to talk, and we had to queue up at her desk if we had a question. Some of the girls had plasters on their fingers and were excused the lesson, so they just sat and watched the others. I overheard one girl say in the playground at break-time that she hated Mrs Bryan's lessons so much that she had deliberately cut her finger at home the night before so that she didn't have to take part in the sewing lesson. I was shocked as I had never come across anyone doing anything like this to avoid a lesson.

On the second Friday that I was at the school, the girls again played Vigaro. Mr Deasey insisted this time that I should join in. I was picked last and with obvious reluctance, but I was determined to show them that I could be an asset to the team. I scored one or two runs, not really understanding the rules, and then the girl at the other end, Dawn, hit the ball and started to run to my end, so I took off for the other end, only to have the ball fielded quickly and I was stumped out before I reached the crease. Dawn immediately walked down the wicket and offered me her bat ... and I had no idea why. I realise now that it was a polite way of saying 'I'm sorry I caused you to be run out', and that the bat should always be declined but I had not been told the rules so I didn't understand what was going on and just stood there with two bats in my hand asking "*What do I do now?*". I was conscious of stares of disbelief from the other girls, and eventually the next girl due to bat walked over to me, snatched one of the bats out of my hand and spat out the words "*Get up the other end!*". Confused, because I thought I was out, I did as I was told. At the end of the game, they all kept saying what a rotten sport I was and how awful it was that I accepted the bat from Dawn. I was mortified and cried all the way home.

Mum could see that I was upset when she got home, but as we were babysitting again on both Friday and Saturday nights, she didn't have much time for sympathy. When we got to the Lethbridges it was a fine evening, so the girls and Phippa had their bicycles out in the garden. I watched them and thought "*I can do that, it looks easy*", so I couldn't wait to start learning on my own bike. The babysitting was uneventful again and the Lethbridges seemed pleased with the way we carried out our duties – I used to read Phippa a story and tuck him up into bed. He was such a good boy and the girls also behaved impeccably. The money certainly came in handy and

Mum was able to gradually buy items to make our life more comfortable. She made sure that I was repaid the ten shillings that I had given her for food as soon as she had the money to spare.

On Saturday morning Mum took me out onto the street, the surface of which was gravel and sand, for my first cycling lesson. I was brimming with confidence, swung my leg over the crossbar, and with Mum holding onto the saddle I started my wobbly progress up the street. When Mum thought I had got my balance, she let go. Within seconds I was flat on my side with gravel rash up my leg. The problem seemed to be that, once I felt that I was falling, I was unable to get my leg over the crossbar in order to jump off to save me from falling sideways. My legs ended up with grazes all over them, but worse than that was the comments from the audience that I had attracted. Children had come out of the surrounding houses to watch, and they laughed when I fell off, but what was more humiliating than that was the comments I got … "*Look at her, bloody pommy, she is so stupid she doesn't know a boy's bike from a girl's bike!*". I was mortified – the bicycle that I was so proud of half an hour ago had now become a monstrosity in my eyes and I never wanted to ride it again. It had never occurred to me that a boy's bike would attract such derision. To me, a bike was a bike. Mum and I went in the garage, and she gave me a cuddle and put antiseptic ointment on my legs. She explained gently that there was no possibility of replacing the bike, and I would have to get used to it. For the next few days I only practised when it was dark, and eventually I was able to ride the bike with no problem. Everyone got used to seeing me on it and the comments lessened off. At least I **had** a bike – some of the children who catcalled didn't, so I eventually felt slightly superior to them anyway.

On Monday I walked to school with the Hornseys, and had a reasonably uneventful day until afternoon playtime. I sat in the shelter watching the girls throw their balls up at the beam, when a pretty girl came and sat next to me. She had dark hair in beautiful long plaits and she had a ball in her hand. *"Would you like to play ball with me?"*, she asked. She told me that her name was Brenda Howard, and that her Father was English. This was the start of a lifelong friendship which has lasted to this day. I was not very good at the ball game at first, but gradually improved with practice. From then on we played every break time – what a difference this friendship made to my life! The other girls were still ignoring me and being rude at every opportunity, but Brenda was a firm and loyal friend and I was, and still am, truly grateful to her for being brave enough to break down some of the barriers.

I couldn't wait to tell Mum about Brenda, and she was thrilled for me. As we sat talking about it there was a knock at the door. A tall, handsome gentleman asked if Mum was Mrs Baker. He explained that he was a friend of the Lethbridges and that they had highly recommended Mum as a babysitter. His name was Mr Ferguson and he owned a vineyard near Rutherglen, about 7 miles outside of Corowa. He said he was prepared to pay Mum the same hourly rate as the Lethbridges, and asked if we could babysit his children for them over the following weekend. Mum said she would be delighted, but only if the Lethbridges didn't need us. Mr Ferguson said he had already cleared that with Mr Lethbridge, so Mum agreed to do it. He arranged to pick us up on Saturday afternoon, we were to stay overnight and he would bring us back on the Sunday evening. He said that he and his wife were going to stay with friends over the weekend, but that he had a cook, so Mum would not need to prepare any meals ... this came as a great relief to Mum! So started another four-year babysitting commitment to a lovely family who treated us with respect.

Life settled down into a routine during the next few weeks. My friendship with Brenda made school bearable; in Sewing Class I had suffered the lash of Mrs Bryan's tongue, (and I even considered just putting a plaster on my finger to get out of Sewing lessons!) but I had finally completed a pretty apron which I gave to Mum; I was doing well in all academic subjects which still made me the target of the other children; I had mastered the rules of Vigaro and was proving to be a worthy team member although I was still always selected last; and I was getting quite adept at the ball game with Brenda in the shelter.

One day Brenda invited me to her house for tea. We went straight from school and I was introduced to her Mum and Dad, and her younger sister Betty. She also had an older brother John, and an older sister Joyce, both of whom I met on other visits to her house. Tea was divine – Brenda's Mum was a superb cook and after Mum's cooking it was heaven, the highlight of my visits. I never mentioned this to Mum, though! Brenda's Dad was one of three brothers who had emigrated from England, married Australian girls and settled in Corowa. Brenda loved horses and eventually she got one of her own, Trixie, which she often let me ride, teaching me all the skills I needed to stay in the saddle. When she was riding I would ride my bike alongside and she would do the same if I was riding Trixie. Brenda's friendship, kindness and generosity meant all the world to me – she was still the only girl in the school who would willingly associate with me, and she made my life bearable. Mum was delighted that I had found such a good friend and she eventually met Brenda's family. We spent many happy hours in their company – and Mum came to appreciate just how excellent Mrs Howard's cooking was!

Chapter 15 – More Babysitting

When Mum got home from work one day she said she had some good news, that we would be babysitting again for the Lethbridges that evening. She had also been paid her first wages and she said that we would go shopping on Saturday morning to get some of the things we needed. Mr Lethbridge picked us up and the evening was uneventful, the children behaving beautifully. This weekend babysitting job was to become a regular commitment, sometimes we even stayed for the weekend when Mr and Mrs Lethbridge went away on golfing weekends – I got on well with the children and Mum took her responsibilities very seriously, so the Lethbridges came to trust her completely. They would leave money and valuable jewellery lying around the house, knowing that it would not be touched. The extra income was a godsend and allowed us to buy the necessities – and we were extremely grateful to them for treating us like human beings.

On the Saturday morning Mum and I walked to Sanger Street and bought me some school blouses (Mrs

Hornsey had completed the second gym slip, so I was now able to wear the full school uniform). Then we had a little spending-spree on household items like more bed linen, writing paper and pen, an iron and ironing board, a broom and dustpan, a mop and bucket, a hammer, nails and screwdriver, but most exciting of all, Mum bought a length of material and some stretchy curtain wires. We arrived home with our purchases and after lunch we sat together outside in the sunshine, stitching by hand some curtains for the little window and a much larger matching curtain to divide the bed area off from the kitchen area. I climbed up on the chair and fixed the curtain wires up and we stood back to admire our handiwork. The long curtain wire across the garage sagged threateningly in the middle, which made Mum and I laugh, but an extra nail in the roof solved that problem and we were very proud of our room divider! The little window was a louvre window, with fly netting on the outside, and the curtains made the garage look very cheerful. After this was done Mum sat down and wrote a long letter to Peter, and a long letter to Joanie and Fred telling them all about the treatment we had received and what a dreadful place Australia was for English people.

I suddenly remembered the 'lecturette' that I was to give, and I told Mum about it, explaining how frightened I was of standing out in front of the class. I asked her what I should talk about, as the girls and boys showed no signs of wanting to know anything about England, the subject that I knew most about. Mum suggested that I talk about the boat trip. She said that none of them would have done anything like that, so they should find it interesting. I was thrilled with this suggestion ... why didn't I think of that? I spent the next couple of days preparing it, rehearsing it to Mum until I was confident of what I had to say and confident that I wouldn't dry up before the three minutes was up.

On Sunday morning Mum said we were going to go to Church. We walked to St John's Church on the Deniliquin Road and went into Morning Prayer. When we came out, we shook hands with the Rector and then we went for a walk down to the bottom of Sanger Street, past the Terminus Hotel and along the road towards the Foord Bridge across the river. The bridge was preceded by a long stretch of boarded road – this had been built to cross the flood plain of the river. The road was bordered by lovely old gum trees and it was quite a pretty area. When we got to the bridge, on the right-hand side we saw lots of people sitting on the bank of the river by an old boat house – we learned later that this area was called the Boatshed. Some were swimming, the children swinging out on a rope hung from a gum tree whose branches stretched out over the water, and dipped into it. Some people were picnicking and it was obviously a popular spot. The river was really wide at this point, probably a quarter of a mile, and on the other side the banks were covered in willow trees. The willow trees reminded us of England – we sat on the bank for a while, both of us feeling really homesick, and then we headed for home. Mum promised we would bring a picnic to this place when we had time.

We walked back to the garage and had lunch. After that, we sat outside reading and then we walked back to the Church for Evening Prayer. As we left the Church, the Rector again shook hands with us, but this time he said to Mum "*I noticed you in Church this morning, and wondered if you are new to the area, or just here on holiday?*". Mum told him that we had just moved into Corowa, without elaborating, and he invited her to join the Mothers' Union. This was held once a week in the Church Hall across the road, so Mum said she would come along and try one of the meetings. The Rector was Canon Ross-Edwards, and we would come to know him well. Then we wandered home, had some tea, and went to bed early, ready for work and school the next day.

Mum tried the Mothers' Union meeting the following week, and she enjoyed it. She said they were polite to her, and so she felt accepted. She met a lady called Mrs Maclean, and once they got to know each other they became firm friends, a friendship that lasted many, many years until Mrs Maclean died. I stayed at home whilst Mum went to these meetings and either went up to the Hornsey's house to play games with the children, or took Lizzie, the black Cocker Spaniel for a walk. Sometimes Tessie, Shirley and I would cycle to Rutherglen across the Foord Bridge, but the problem with this was, during the nesting season, the big black and white magpies would get very aggressive and swoop down at you, trying to peck you – many are the times that I fell off my bike trying to avoid their spiteful beaks and flapping wings!

The day arrived for me to give my 'lecturette'. I was really nervous, but fortunately I wasn't the first to have to do it. There were three ahead of me – 'My Pets'; 'How to make a Model Aeroplane'; and 'My Garden'. The first was a girl who spoke about her dog, her cats, and her Sulphur Crested cockatoo that could talk. The children listened with interest, asked her a few questions, and she was awarded seven points out of ten. The second one, a boy, explained how he cut out the pieces for his aeroplanes from balsa wood, glued them together, and hung then from his bedroom ceiling when they were finished – oh, how this brought back memories of the happy days in Peckham when Peter had done exactly the same thing! Again, the children were interested and asked some questions, and Mr Deasey awarded him seven out of ten also. Then a girl talked about the piece of garden that her Father had given her, where she grew some vegetables and flowers. She talked about how she had prepared the soil, then planted the seeds and eventually harvested the vegetables. The class was fascinated, and asked her a lot of questions, so she was awarded eight out of ten. Now it was my turn. Trembling, I started to describe the trip from England, starting at boarding the boat, through all the ports we stopped at, all the marvellous things we had seen, and finally arriving in Melbourne. I noticed whilst I was speaking that the children looked bored, and when I had finished Mr Deasey asked if anyone had a question. There was complete silence … surely at least **one** of them would be curious about this trip? Mr Deasey asked why there were no questions, and a girl put her hand up and said it was very boring because they had heard it all before from Robert Clark, one of the English boys, and why couldn't I choose something **interesting** to talk about? I was devastated, I had been so sure that it would be a success. How could I possibly know that Robert had chosen the same subject when he gave his 'lecturette'? Mr Deasey awarded me two out of ten and dismissed the class. I fled home and sobbed until Mum came home from work. When would I ever get things right at school?

She comforted me, told me that I was her little star and that if she didn't have me with her she wouldn't be able to cope, which made me feel much better.

After a couple of weeks attending Mothers' Union meetings, Mum asked if there was a Brownie Pack in Corowa, as she thought it would be good for me to join something like that. She found out that there wasn't one as there was no-one prepared to take it on. Mum mentioned that she had been Tawny Owl to a pack in London, and as soon as the Rector heard that he called on Mum at the garage and asked her would she consider starting up a Brownie Pack in Corowa. I think Mum was quite flattered at being asked and she readily accepted. A notice was posted in the Church Hall about it, the necessary papers were obtained from the Girl Guide Movement, and the first night arrived ... only two girls and I turned up! However, word got round and soon there were more and more turning up until Mum had a thriving Brownie pack, even though there was no volunteer to fill the requirement for a Tawny Owl. I received no different treatment from Mum to all the other Brownies, which I think helped get rid of some of the resentment they felt. It turned out to be a very successful Pack. One day I came back from lunch to see a girl who was a member of the Brownie Pack waddling along doing a funny walk. I laughed along with the others, who looked a bit sheepish. Maureen immediately stopped when she realised I was there. I found out some time later that she had been mimicking Mum and it really hurt my feelings to think that anyone could be so cruel, especially as Mum was working hard to make a success of the Brownie Pack.

I had been thinking about the 'lecturette' given by the girl on 'My Pets', and wished I too could have a pet. We had discovered an old birdcage behind the garage, so Mum asked Mrs Hornsey if we could have a parrot. Vincent attached the cage to the side wall outside the garage for us. A man who lived opposite sold baby galahs, an Australian grey parrot with a pink underbelly, so we bought one and he was christened 'Cocky'. We had seen flocks of these birds flying overhead like a blazing pink cloud and making a lot of noise. 'Cocky' made a good pet and eventually was able to say a passable imitation of his name, answering us when we spoke to him. I was responsible for cleaning his cage, making sure he had food and water, and I loved him. I also managed to achieve my Brownie Badge in Pet Care, so I was very proud of that.

During this time we had been babysitting for the Lethbridges a lot, and Mum was getting regular wages from her work, so she wondered if we could find better accommodation. We followed up all the leads that we received regarding accommodation for rent … but it was always the same, either an outright blatantly rude rejection, or a frosty "*The accommodation is already taken*" when we knew it was not. We resigned ourselves to staying where we were, and gradually Mum bought more and more items to make our life more comfortable. For instance, she bought two single beds and returned the fold-up one to Mrs Hornsey. She bought a food storage unit called a meat safe that had a sort of metal mesh with small round holes in it at the sides and across the top, with a wooden bottom, 3 shelves and wooden legs on it about eight inches high. Unfortunately, the first morning we went to get food out it was crawling with small black ants. Most of the food was salvageable, and when Mum told the other girls at work what had happened, they laughed and said she must stand the feet in lids from jam jars filled with paraffin. She did this that evening ... problem solved, so long as you kept the paraffin topped up!

The winter had really set in by now, and Mum was busy knitting garments to keep us warm. She asked the girls at work for any spare wool that they had left over, and she knitted me a 'coat of many colours' from the remnants, a lovely stripey cardigan. The first time that I wore it to school I earned the nickname 'Joseph', but I had nothing else warm to wear, so in the end the children just got used to it and stopped teasing me about it.

One day there was great excitement when Mum got home from work – Mrs Hornsey gave Mum a letter that had arrived in the mail that day, and we were thrilled to see that it was from Peter. At last, some news!

Chapter 16 – Letters!

Mum's hands were trembling as she opened the envelope. Inside was a long letter from Peter ... but it was not from Berrigan, but a farm near Mulwala, 30 miles away. Peter explained that he had fallen in love with Lorraine, the daughter of the farmer at Berrigan where he had been employed, and he had asked her Father if they could get married. When her Father heard this he was very angry, told Peter that there was no way he was going to let his daughter marry a 'pommy bastard' (this being to us a new and nastier version of the old insult), and that he had 24 hours to get off the property as he was no longer prepared to sponsor him under the 'Big Brother' scheme. Peter said he was very shocked at this response, and that he had not been allowed to speak to Lorraine before he had left. (Now we knew what the 'problem' was referred to by the farmer who had sponsored Mum). Not knowing what to do, Peter had hitch-hiked to the farm where Sid, his friend from the ship, was still a 'Little Brother', and the farmer there had taken Peter on as a farm hand. He fortunately had received Mum's letter before he was made to leave Berrigan, but events had moved so quickly that this was the first chance he had had to reply. In a strange irony, Peter had been treated better by his new employer than he had been under the scheme that was supposed to help and protect young men, and he was being paid a proper wage with reasonable accommodation. This later caused Sid some discontent, because he was still being treated pretty much like a slave whilst he was under his 'Big Brother' contract, but for now they were getting on well together.

Peter said that he had been shaken to the core when he had heard what had happened to Mum and me, but he had no money and was in no position to help us. He was obviously experiencing a huge guilty conscience for encouraging us to come to Australia and said he would never forgive himself for being the cause of so much suffering. He said he still loved Lorraine, but that he knew he had no chance with her, so he had immersed himself in his work and was saving hard to buy a car.

Mum sat down immediately after tea and replied to Peter's letter, which had taken three weeks to get to us. She told him that the split between Peter and Lorraine had probably been for the best as he would never have been accepted into her family, bearing in mind the deep prejudices against English people that these farmers had. She also told him that he must not blame himself for what had happened to us, nobody could have predicted it, and anyway, we were now quite comfortably settled, she had a good job and I was doing well at school. She said that she hoped that, if he got a car, he might visit us if he got the chance. The letter was duly sent, and I for one couldn't wait to hear from him again.

On the weekends when we were not babysitting, Mum and I would go to Church twice on a Sunday. Once a month there would be a Brownie Parade at Morning Prayer, and the Brownie Pack now had about 30 girls in it. Mum would take them on picnics to the Boatshed and on nature rambles, learning all she could about the local flora and fauna from library books. Mum had been a Swimming Instructress at the Victoria Baths in Manchester in her youth, so she taught a lot of the Brownies to swim at the Boatshed. I had learned to swim at an early age and was very soon swimming the quarter of a mile across the river with Mum to The Willows on the Wahgunyah side and back. When I mentioned that Mum and I regularly swum across the river and back at school, the girls told me that there was a fish in the river called the Redfin which had a huge spiny fin on its back, and that they would get underneath you in the water and rip your stomach open with the fin. This terrified me and it was some time before I returned to swimming at the Boatshed! There was indeed a fish called the Redfin in the Murray River and it did have a sharp fin on top, but I have never heard of anyone being injured by one, so I think it was just one of those old wives' tales that people, especially children, loved repeating.

Mum was keen to re-introduce me to piano lessons and when she was earning the extra money from babysitting she investigated the possibility of finding a local piano teacher. She was told that there was one near St John's Church and despite my protestations that I couldn't play she arranged for me to meet her from work one day and we went to the house on the Deniliquin Road where the piano teacher lived. The door was opened by a short, chubby lady, who invited us in. She asked me what stage I was up to, and had I taken any examinations. I told her the level I had achieved in England (but I didn't mention that it was only because I got rapped on the knuckles with a ruler, not because I had any talent for music!), and she agreed to take me on. My first lesson was the following week and she got very impatient with my lack of ability. It had been several months since I had even touched a piano so I had forgotten everything I had learned in England. I told Mum when I got home that I had not got on very well, but she insisted that I persevere. On the following Sunday Mum asked the Rector if he knew of anyone who had a piano that I could use to practise on. This was a crafty move on her behalf, as she had noticed a piano in the Church Hall when she had taken Brownie meetings in there. Of course, the Rector readily offered the use of this piano and it was arranged that I would collect the key from the Rectory whenever I wanted to practise. When I went to my next lesson I told the teacher that I had somewhere to practise, so she said that I had better start right away as I really needed it. Then, horror of horrors, she picked up a wooden ruler and sat there as I played, rapping me on the knuckles when I hit a wrong note. I couldn't believe that I had managed to escape the sadist in England who did this, and here was another teacher doing the same thing – I think they must have learned their methods from the same training manual! (The end result of this was that I passed several examinations over the next year up to the stage where you no longer had set pieces, and then my musical career came to an end. I am still not able to read music, and can't even play 'Chopsticks', which most children can manage without even concentrating!). I used to go every day after school to the Church Hall to practise whilst I was going to lessons, and my little green bike stood me in good stead for getting around. I would leave it outside the Church Hall but word got round that I was using the piano in there, and I would come out to find that my bike had been urinated on, or dog's excrement had been smeared on the saddle, or it had been hidden somewhere different to where I left it. Sometimes there would be a note in a child's handwriting saying 'Go back to where you came from, you bloody pommy', and on one occasion a pedal had been stolen. Fortunately, being a fixed wheel bicycle I was able to ride it home using one pedal, and Vincent repaired it for me. Not only were my piano lessons awful, but I was beginning to dread going to the Church Hall to practise, never knowing what I would find when I came out. Mum told the Rector what was going on and he promised to keep an eye open for who was doing these horrid things, but he was a busy man and not always able to do this. The tormenting continued and one day I came out of the hall and was thrilled to find my bike untouched, but as I got on it to ride away, some boys came from behind and spat at me, saying "*Go home, bloody pommy*". I didn't recognise the voices and I was so frightened I pedalled off without turning round to look at them. When I got home and told Mum, we went straight to the Rectory to tell the Rector who promised to keep a closer eye on me. The very next time I was in the hall I heard a commotion outside but didn't dare go out. Eventually the Rector came into the hall and said he had caught three boys damaging my bike, that he had got their names and he was going to see their parents.

When I got outside, I cried my eyes out at the state of my bike – the tyres had been slashed, a pedal was lying nearby and the mudguards had been twisted sideways. I carried the bicycle home, crying all the way. Mum was livid when she saw it; the next time she saw the Rector he told her that he had seen the boys' parents and if we took the bike to Cyril Dungey's, the bicycle shop in the town, he would repair it and the parents would reimburse us. I have to say that I am very ashamed of what I did next. I took the bike to Cyril Dungey's and he repaired it. I collected it and paid two shillings and sixpence for the repairs. On the way up to the address that the Rector had given us, I passed a jeweller's shop, and saw a pretty necklace in the window for twelve shillings and sixpence. I decided to say that the bike cost twelve shillings and sixpence to repair, then go straight away and buy Mum the necklace to cheer her up after all the trauma she had been through. I knocked on the door, told the man who I was and told him that the bike had cost twelve shillings and sixpence. He told me to come back the next day for the money. I should have learned when I was caught stealing the ten shilling note out of Joanie's money box that being dishonest never pays! When I got home Mum was pleased to see that the bike was fixed and I told her that I had to return the next day for the money. When we were having tea, there was a knock on the door – it was the Rector. He asked me to wait outside whilst he spoke with Mum. Then I was told to come back inside and I found Mum in tears. Apparently the boy's Father had thought that twelve shillings and sixpence was excessive so he had gone to Cyril Dungey's to ask why he had charged so much. On being told that he had only charged two shillings and sixpence, the boy's father was incensed, so he went straight to the Rector and told him what had happened. The Rector looked at me very sternly, and asked me why I had lied about the price. By this time I was crying too so I told him about the necklace. He said he was very disappointed in me and told me never to do anything like that again. As an afterthought he said to me "*From now on you must take your bicycle into the hall with you whenever you are there*" and then he left. I thought Mum was going to give me a hiding, but the sadness reflected in her eyes was punishment enough. She told me that I had to pay the two shillings and sixpence out of my pocket money over the next five weeks. That really was the last time I ever did anything deliberately dishonest – and when I had finished paying back Mum for the repairs I saved up my pocket money and finally bought Mum the necklace some time later.

A few days later when Mum got home from work, Mrs Hornsey gave her another letter. Mum came into the garage, held the letter up high and said "*Guess who this is from!*". I thought that I knew straight away, and shouted "*Peter!*". "*Wrong,*" said Mum, "*it's from Joanie!*". My heart missed a beat, so much had happened since we last heard from Joanie, and now we had news of what she had been doing since we left England. I sat on Mum's lap as we read the letter together, and as the words revealed themselves on the page, Mum's tears started to fall. Joanie dropped a bombshell – she and Fred had decided that there would not be much of a future for them in London so they too had applied to Australia House and been accepted as emigrants to Australia, destined for Sydney. They had been told that they didn't need a sponsor because they were due to go into a hostel in Sydney, where Fred would take his turn at the jobs that were offered to the immigrants there (usually quite menial, manual work). Mum's letter telling them how horrible it had been for us had arrived too late to stop the whole process and they were due to arrive in late August, on the SS Ormonde (15,000 tons). Mum was devastated – the last thing she wanted was for Joanie and Fred to go through what we had been experiencing. To make matters worse, we had read reports in the newspapers about the hostels in Sydney. There, young couples were separated, segregated into male and female hostels, seeing each other infrequently, and some had to stay there for months before they had been able to get employment. The living conditions were dreadful and the last thing that Mum wanted was for this to happen to Joanie and Fred. We were then in early July and they were due to arrive in the third week of August. Mum knew that there was no point in writing back to Joanie as she and Fred would be leaving before any letter would be delivered to them. The fear that they were doing the wrong thing was somewhat mitigated by the thought of seeing them both again. I for one couldn't wait, but Mum was filled with trepidation on their behalf. She began to devise a plan to resolve the situation.

Chapter 17– Joyful Reunions

I came home from piano practice one day shortly after we had received Joanie's letter and there was a car parked outside, a black Triumph Mayflower. Several children were standing near the back of it, writing 'This car needs cleaning' in the dust on the boot. When they saw me approaching on my bike they scooted away in all directions. I assumed that Mr Hall next door had visitors, so I thought it was quite funny. I walked down to the garage, in through the door, and there, with the biggest grin on his face that you could imagine, stood my beloved brother, Peter, my hero! This was not the skinny young boy that I had said goodbye to on the ship the previous year – this was a tanned, handsome man, taller and more muscular than before. He swept me up in his arms and gave me the biggest hug in the world. I was **so** happy to see him, it was like a dream come true. Mum was smiling from ear to ear also as she started to cook us some tea. Peter explained that he had finally saved enough money to buy a car and managed to take some time off from his farm work, so he had headed straight for Corowa. Mum had already told him the news about Joanie and Fred and he was so pleased to hear that the family would all be together again soon.

Peter decided that he would bring his car into the driveway so we walked down to the big gate together. I suddenly remembered what the children had done to the car and told Peter about them. He was really angry, as the dust that had settled on the car from his journey was gritty and where the children had written in it there were many scratches where they had pushed the grit across the paintwork. I felt guilty as I had seen it happen and thought it quite funny, but he gave me a hug and said it would have been much worse if I hadn't disturbed them. He moved the car into the drive; we ate tea and then sat talking until very late. There was so much to catch up on, so many things to be said. Mum told him not to feel guilty about us, or indeed about Joanie and Fred, it would all turn out alright. Mum and I slept in one bed, Peter slept in the other one and we all went to sleep feeling happier than we had for a very long time.

Mrs Hornsey knocked on the door as Peter was getting ready to leave early the next morning. She stood there with her hands on her hips and an accusing look on her face. I think she thought that Mum had a boyfriend staying overnight, but when she was introduced to Peter she realised that her suspicions were unfounded and was obviously won over by this handsome, polite stranger. Peter had to return to work that day and he promised to write regularly. When he left we walked to the car all together and said our farewells. When Peter saw my tears, he reassured me that now he had a car, he would come as often as he could.

The Hornseys kept some chooks (chickens) on a piece of land that was separated from their garden by a thick hedge; the flies seemed to like the chooks as much as they liked the horses next door, so they were a constant problem. Mum was still suffering badly with the heat as it was getting warmer as the year progressed. The Lethbridges recommended an odd-job man to Mum, who after Mum had asked Mrs Hornsey for permission, came and fitted a fly screen to the door of the garage and also cut another window complete with louvres and fly screen in the 'living' end to give us some light and ventilation there. It made such a difference having some fresh air, as the door had been kept shut to keep the flies out most of the time. Mum and I stitched another pair of curtains for the new window and I think she was secretly quite proud of the way she had turned a garage into a passable home for us both.

On one occasion the Hornseys were killing off some of the older hens for meat – they made no fuss about this, Vincent just chopped off the heads on the block that they used to chop their wood on. Sometimes the chooks kept on flapping once the head was removed and I always found this quite scary, but when they said we could have a chicken provided **I** cut the head off, I decided to do it. I wielded the axe and brought it down cleanly on the neck of the chicken and when I let go of the chicken it ran a few yards. This nearly made me sick, but I got used to doing it and eventually could perform this task without batting an eyelid. Mum and I plucked and cleaned the chicken and it was then boiled in the saucepan, providing us with a bit of variety to our diet.

We had received one letter from Joanie after the first one that told us they were coming and this one told us about the first days on board ship, when Joanie had been very seasick, but Fred was alright – the dreaded Bay of Biscay again! Mum had obviously given a lot of thought to the fact that Joanie and Fred were going to have to end up in Sydney in awful segregated accommodation and one day in mid-August she said to me "*I am not going to let Joanie and Fred go to Sydney. We will go to Melbourne and take them off the boat*". I didn't believe that she could do this, but she saved every penny she could and the day before they were due to arrive we caught the train to Melbourne from Corowa. When we arrived in Melbourne we caught the tram to the Travellers' Aid, where the girls from our cabin had stayed, and booked in for the night. We were accommodated in a dormitory of twelve beds … and I spent most of the night thinking about seeing my darling sister again until I eventually fell into a fitful sleep.

The next morning we went to the docks and just before lunchtime we sat and watched as the SS Ormonde docked. It was always impressive watching these huge ships 'park' alongside the quay, but this time my heart was thumping with excitement at the thought of seeing Joanie and Fred again. After the gangway was lowered we watched the passengers – some looking excited, some looking nervous and some looking downright scared – disembarking. We scanned their faces to see if Joanie and Fred had decided to have a look at Melbourne, but there was no sign of them so Mum and I walked up the gangway. Once we were on the boat she approached the first Officer she saw and demanded, yes, demanded to be taken to the Captain! She explained that she had a request. Mum was able to be quite a dominant figure when she wanted something very much – the Officer was so taken aback he asked us to follow him! When we reached the door to the crew's quarters, he asked us to wait. After about 10 minutes he returned and escorted us through the corridor to the Captain's office. The Captain was seated at his desk and he asked Mum what she wanted. As soon as she started to explain that her daughter and son-in-law were passengers on the ship he was very surprised, as he had assumed that we were passengers on the ship, not visitors. Mum told him that she wanted to take Joanie and Fred off the ship right now! She was not going to allow them to go on to Sydney and she was not going to argue about it. The Captain was taken aback, but after some thought he told Mum that the fare had been paid to take them to Sydney so it didn't really matter to him whether they completed the journey or not. He looked up their two cabin numbers (all emigrants in economy class were segregated on board, even the married ones), and then pressed a buzzer on his desk. A sailor appeared and the Captain asked him to prepare a short document for Mum to sign saying that she accepted full responsibility for removing them from his ship. He checked the cargo sheets and told Mum that Mr and Mrs Brehme had no hold luggage, which made things a lot easier. It did not surprise Mum, as Joanie and Fred had lived with Fred's Mum since they married so they had no furniture of their own, not even kitchen equipment, so they had just brought clothes and personal items with them. The sailor re-appeared with a piece of paper and Mum couldn't sign it quickly enough. Then the Captain asked the sailor to take us to Joanie's cabin; after shaking the Captain's hand and thanking him profusely we followed the sailor out into the corridor. My heart was beating fit to burst as we made our way down into the 'bowels' of the ship, to a similar cabin to the one that we had occupied with the four girls on our trip. Mum knocked on the door as I held my breath. Joanie opened the door, gasped, and enfolded us in her arms. She was speechless, and so was Mum and they held each other tightly as if they would never let go again. Fred stood behind her and I was thrilled to hear him say "*Hello, Titch, what on earth are you doing here?*". I hugged them both, tears running down my face. It seemed so much more than five months since we had seen them, so much had happened to us in that short time. Then it all tumbled out and they were both shocked and pleased when they heard what Mum had done. They too had heard the stories on board about the hostels in Sydney and they were anticipating their arrival there with trepidation. Fred returned to his cabin to pack (they had both been in the same cabin when we arrived because the other occupants had left the ship to explore Melbourne, and Joanie and Fred were taking advantage of the fact that they could have the cabin to themselves for a while, having had very little time to be alone together on the journey. The significance of this escaped me; after all, I was only ten years old and very innocent!). Joanie packed her things and wrote a quick note to her cabin mates explaining what had happened. She included our address in the note so that they could keep in touch. Then our group of four happy people made their way down the gangway and onto a tram to the Travellers' Aid. When we booked in for the night, poor Fred had again to be segregated from us females so he was allocated a bed in a male dormitory.

The next morning we caught the train back to Corowa and Joanie's and Fred's eyes widened with every new sight they saw as they made the journey that they could have in no way anticipated. Fred was very quiet and I sensed that, having come from a large, close-knit family, he was already missing his Mum and brothers and sisters. We described the garage to them both but I don't think they really grasped the picture too well.

We eventually arrived at Corowa and it was not too long a walk to Walker Street. Joanie and Fred walked into the garage, put their cases down, and Joanie burst into tears. Mum thought that it was because she didn't like the garage, but she told us that she was shocked to see what we had had to put up with. Once the tears were over we made some tea and listened whilst they told us all about the journey. Joanie had got over her seasickness and they had both enjoyed the trip apart from being separated at night. When they realised that they would be sleeping in a single bed I think they were quite pleased at the thought of being able to cuddle up, but Mum pointed out that it would be in the same room as Mum and me in the other bed, which sort of dampened their enthusiasm! Mum then took them up to meet Mrs Hornsey, who had already agreed that they could stay with us until they found their own place.

Mum had spoken to Mr Strong about Joanie and asked if there was any possibility that the firm might be able to find a job for her. They had agreed to interview her, so two days later Joanie went with Mum to the office, took a typing and shorthand test and came home with a job! She was thrilled, as the prospects of a reasonable job in Sydney had been practically nil, and she had been expecting to be unemployed for some time. Freddie scanned the newspapers for job adverts, applied for several ... and it was no surprise that he was rejected every time. Sometimes he received the 'job taken' reply, sometimes it was a blatantly rude refusal to employ a 'bloody pommy'. We had warned him that this would be the case, but I don't think he expected it to be quite so vindictive. Then there was a breakthrough – one of the ladies at the Mothers' Union meetings was married to the Maintenance Engineer at the hospital and he needed an assistant. As Fred had worked all his life since leaving school for Evans Lifts, he was highly skilled in maintenance and engineering work, so he attended the hospital for an interview and came home triumphant, having been offered a job starting the following Monday. We were all delighted – the outcome of bringing Joanie and Fred back to Corowa with us was exceeding all expectations.

However, with all of us living in a small space, there were lots of disadvantages. Joanie and Fred had no time to themselves, slept in a single bed, and as Fred was working shifts he was coming in at different times and disturbing us during the night, or he was trying to sleep during the day when it was impossible for us to be perfectly quiet in such a small space, especially at the weekends. He was finding it difficult to sleep with the noise of Mr Hall breaking in the horses next door, too.

Mum and Joanie had bought some material and another curtain was made to separate the two beds down the middle to give a little more privacy. Each bed occupied most of the space, so getting undressed and dressed was a real challenge! This fired Joanie and Fred's efforts to find their own accommodation, but to no avail. Every time they went to enquire about advertised rooms to let, they were given the 'bloody pommies' treatment and verbally abused, especially now that word had circulated that they had both been able to find employment so quickly. They were often told "*Go back to where you came from, don't come over here taking jobs that we could have*". Unfortunately, there were a lot of Australians who didn't want to work and the fact that Joanie and Fred had secured jobs showed the Australians in a bad light.

To cheer all of us up, Mum decided to take us all to the pictures. It was the strangest experience because the film that was showing was 'Unknown Island', the scary one about dinosaurs that we had been to see in London on Joanie's 18th birthday. Films that were released in England took about three years to reach the small towns in Australia in those days. At least this time I knew when to close my eyes! The Rex Theatre was at the top end of Sanger Street and opposite it was the Austral open-air ground, used to show pictures in the very hot weather. Sometimes when the film started off in this open-air annexe, the heavens would open with torrential rain, sending everyone scurrying across the road into the proper cinema. This was great for anyone who happened to be in Sanger Street at the time as they could join the crowd filing into the Rex Theatre and see the rest of the film without paying!

Finally, after seven weeks an elderly couple in Whitehead Street, just round the corner from Walker Street, who had advertised a room for rent, accepted

Joanie and Fred on the understanding that they would help around the house with the heavy jobs. We helped them move in two days before Joanie's 21st birthday in early October. Mum had been saving up and on Joanie's birthday Mum presented her with a brand new bicycle. She was thrilled to bits now that she had a means of getting about other than walking. The bigger surprise was that Mum bought herself a bicycle too – now it was only Fred who needed transport.

Fred finally got himself a bicycle and he also bought a ·22 calibre rifle to shoot rabbits with. At first the idea was to shoot them for food, but when he discovered that mixamatosis was rife in the Australian rabbit he decided just to shoot them for sport. There was an abandoned gold mine just outside of Corowa where a huge mound of earth from the mine was piled up, and we used to cycle out there and lay full length on the ground, waiting for the rabbits to appear from their burrows in the mound. I was often allowed to use the gun and on one occasion I lay waiting for my target to appear. Directly in front of my nose a small circle of earth was lifted up and out popped a trapdoor spider. I have never been so terrified in all my life – I leapt up, threw the rifle on the ground, grabbed my bicycle and pedalled home as fast as I could ... leaving the others in fits of laughter at my rapidly disappearing figure! I eventually became quite a good shot. We would cut a small hole in the bark of a tree and press a small coin into the hole. Then we would fire at the coin until someone hit it. The coin would then be taken from the tree trunk and a length of cotton would be tied through the hole in the middle of the coin created by the bullet. The cotton would then be tied onto the wire of a fence so that it swung back and forth, and this then became our target. I would hit the swinging coin more times that I missed it, which earned the respect of the adults who couldn't match my scores.

As we approached Guy Fawkes Night, Monday November 5th, we decided that, although we wouldn't be able to have any fireworks (this was not a date that was celebrated in Australia), we would at least have a bonfire and roast some potatoes on it. I was excited, but decided not to tell anyone at school because of the hatred they had for all things English. I came home after school and couldn't wait to enjoy a little bit of 'England' on our own. When everyone was home from work we all walked down to the flood plain close to the river on the other side of the bridge to the Boatshed, and after gathering lots of fallen branches from under the trees we soon had a lovely fire going, a plume of smoke going straight up in the still, breezeless air. Mum had just put the potatoes in the red hot coals when we heard some shouting. In the distance there were several men running towards us, waving branches at us and carrying buckets. Our initial reaction was that they were coming to join our celebration … how wrong we were! They set about us, hitting us with the branches and shouting "*You bloody stupid pommy bastards, get out of here before we kill you*". Fred was the only man with us and would have been unable to take the men on by himself so we all fled, the three of us females sobbing and Fred very angry at not being able to protect us. The men did not chase us, but set about beating out the fire with the branches, and formed a chain to get buckets of water from the river to quench the flames. We hurried all the way back to Walker Street, got into the garage and us three females sat there crying and shaking, wondering what on earth we had done to upset them so. Fred was particularly upset and I think that that was the moment that he decided he was going to get Joanie back to England as soon as he could save up enough for their fares. If you emigrated under the £10 scheme you had to stay in Australia for at least two years, because if you didn't you had to repay the British Government the full cost of the trip out to Australia as well as your own fare back. Fred knew this would be out of the question; he would never be able to afford that, so he knew that spending at least two years in a country that he already despised was going to be tough.

The next day at work, Mum and Joanie related the events of the previous evening to Mr Strong to see if he could shed any light on the reason for the attack. He had no hesitation – didn't we realise that November to March, the hottest time of the Australian summer, was the worst time for bush fires? The sudden enormity of the realisation of what a thoroughly stupid thing we had done made Mum and Joanie feel very embarrassed. How could we have been so unaware of the risk that we were taking? The grass was tinder dry and our fire could have developed into a massive disaster for the town, particularly if there had been a breeze. When Fred heard the explanation that evening, even he was humbled by the thought of what might have happened. It was a lesson to us all and after that we were always conscious of the risks of bushfires and never did anything so stupid again. Unfortunately, the whole town got to hear about it, and 'bloody stupid pommies' became the new taunt.

We apologised profusely to anyone who would listen, but I don't think we were ever forgiven for it.

Chapter 18 – From bad to worse – and back again!

We never did find out whether our stupid actions on Guy Fawkes Day was the cause, but early in December, 1951 both Mum and Joanie were 'laid off' from John Strong's. By this time Fred was highly regarded at the hospital and he was able to talk to the Matron who agreed to take Joanie on as a cleaner. Although this was clearly a waste of her considerable secretarial talents, they needed the money – and the Australians seemed less resentful of an English person having a menial job than occupying a professional post.

Mum, however, was deeply worried about not having an income and knew that she had to find employment quickly. Mrs Maclean, her friend from the Mother's Union, told her that a distant relative of her husband, who had just lost his wife, needed a housekeeper. Mrs Maclean arranged for Mum to have an interview with this Mr Maclean. He lived in Betterment Parade, not too far away from the garage. Mum called round to see him to find out if he would employ her on a non-residential basis, but he refused point blank, and said he needed someone to live in. He told Mum that he had a Cook, and when she heard this Mum decided to take the job, as she couldn't cook well and was relieved that she wouldn't have to do this. Mr Maclean was a tall, upright man in his seventies, and he drove an ancient Bentley, his pride and joy. Mum went to see Mrs Hornsey to explain what had happened. She was very upset because her regular rental payment would come to a halt but when Mum told her that we couldn't take our furniture with us as the room we were to occupy was fully furnished, Mrs Hornsey cheered up a bit as it meant she could rent the garage out to someone else without too much expenditure on it.

Within two days we had moved into Mr Maclean's house, a large, rambling place which was very dark all the time because he refused to have his curtains open, believing the house to be cooler when dark. We took our personal effects and our bikes and said a sad farewell to the garage that had been home to us for over seven months. Mum had not been told at interview but Mr Maclean expected her to cook when the Cook he employed had her days off. She was expected to clean the house and do the washing, ironing and shopping. The inevitable happened ... Mum's domestic skills let her down, and after a month Mr Maclean told Mum that he no longer required her services. It was the first time that I had seen the silent tears for some considerable time.

Mum went straight round to see Mrs Hornsey, praying that she didn't have any tenants in the garage. It was with some irony that Mrs Hornsey told Mum that the garage was still vacant as no Australians would lower themselves to live in a garage. She quite willingly took us back as tenants, knowing by then that Mum would pay her rent as soon as she had another job. We moved our few personal effects back to Walker Street, and apart from being a bit dusty it was as if we had never left. Joanie and Fred were glad that we were closer and more available as Mum had been allowed only one evening off a week when we were at Mr Macleans, and she took Brownies on that evening.

In desperation, Mum went to see if Mr Strong would give her her former job back. He explained that the firm was going through a bad patch, but that he was friendly with the Manager of Maples, the big furniture store at the top end of Sanger Street, and that he was aware that Mr Rippingale needed someone in his office to carry out accounting duties and help in the shop. He said he would put in a good word for Mum. Mr Strong was as good as his word and the following evening he called round to tell Mum that Mr Rippingale would see her the next day.

Nobody could have been more pleased than Mum when she returned home the next day from her interview. Mr Rippingale had been most impressed with her office skills, confident that she could learn book-keeping fairly quickly, and had agreed to take her on from the following Monday. Not only that, but when he learned that Mum and I had babysat for the Lethbridges he asked Mum if she would also babysit for his young sons. Mum said she would when the Lethbridges or the Fergusons didn't need us, and eventually I did most of the babysitting on my own for the Rippingales, giving me some extra pocket money that Mum couldn't afford.

We had not babysat for the Lethbridges for a while and Mum thought that he might have wanted to disassociate himself with us after the bonfire fiasco, but now she wondered if it could just be the fact that his business also was not doing so well and they had curtailed their social activities for a while. However, he also asked us to babysit again the following weekend so once again we had a regular income to cover the outgoings of rent, food and other necessities.

Life seemed to settle into a routine, with all four of us thankful that we had each other. Lizzie, the Hornsey's black Cocker Spaniel, had had puppies and Mum, knowing how much I missed Flossie, said I could have one. I chose a beautiful black male and named him 'Pash'. This was a nickname given to men in the Navy whose surname was Baker and I remembered my Dad telling me that he had always been called by this name. Pash had big paws but none of us actually anticipated just how big a dog he would grow into – I think his dad must have been a Great Dane! Fred built me a kennel and I always took Pash everywhere with me if I could.

On some Saturdays in Corowa there would be a Barn Dance held in the Corowa Literary Institute. The hall would be decked out with gum tree branches, dead rabbits and straw bales. Joanie and Fred used to love the square dances, Mum would dance with Mrs Maclean, and I would sit on the straw bales watching the fun going on but too shy to dance. Some people would dress in fancy dress, some of the men dressing as women, and it would be an evening's enjoyment for everyone.

Christmas arrived, and we celebrated it with a picnic at the Boatshed – it was far too hot to have the traditional turkey dinner, but it seemed really strange for there to be no snow, tinsel and crackers. Fred seemed to feel more homesick than Joanie, Mum or I, but that was understandable. We hadn't heard from Peter for a while and Mum was desperate for some news from him.

The academic year in Australia runs from January to December, with the long summer holiday from before Christmas to nearly the end of January. This meant that I moved up a year at school in January, and we also had a change of Headmaster. The new one was called Mr Turner and he was a drinking, smoking, scruffy individual. I didn't like him and he certainly didn't like me. I was still doing well in all my subjects but Mum felt that he was holding me back, so she had several set-tos with him about my education. His attitude was 'if you don't like the way I teach, teach her yourself'. This was impossible, of course, and I think that the academic year of 1952 was when I lost the advantage of being a year ahead when I first joined the school.

Mrs Bryan again took our Sewing class once a week and we all had to make the sports gym slip that we would need for games at High School the following year. I loved the colours – royal blue material with two yellow stripes right around the skirt just above the hemline, and it was worn with a white blouse and a yellow-gold silky cord with a tassel at both ends. I couldn't wait to wear mine and represent the school in matches. I knew that they played hockey, tennis and basketball (more closely aligned to netball than the American basketball game) and I looked forward so much to leaving behind the hated Vigaro.

In February Corowa held its Annual Show. This was an event that everyone looked forward to. There was something for everyone at the Show, which although mainly agricultural, also had all sorts of stalls, competitions and exhibitions. There were boxing booths, driving competitions, woodmen competitions (where burly men with axes would race to scale a tall pole, creating platforms to stand on as they worked their way up to the top), sheep shearing competitions, the animal judging and all manner of entertainment. Everyone bought or made new clothes and the ladies always wore big picture hats and long gloves. It was a time of escape from the everyday problems of life and I loved the atmosphere of it all.

Looking back, there was an amusing incident which I was unable to appreciate the humour of at the time. I was working on a project at school which required the use of Sellotape ... except that in Australia it was called 'Durex Tape', or 'Durex' for short. When Mum got home from work one night, we went round to see Joanie and Fred and have tea with them. In the middle of the meal I remembered that I needed the tape so I innocently asked Mum "*Will you buy me some Durex to use at school, please?*". I could have in no way predicted the reaction to my simple question! Fred choked and spluttered on his cup of tea and had to leave the room, Joanie looked at me in horror, and Mum went completely white! "*What on earth do you need them for?*", Mum asked angrily. I was puzzled by the reference to 'them' so I said "*I only need one reel to stick things into my book with*". Thankfully the word 'reel' made Mum question me more closely on what I needed, and once I had described the sticky transparent tape she knew what I meant ... but she had no idea that it was called 'Durex Tape' in Australia. I heard her say to Joanie after tea that she thought at first that Mr Turner had decided to give us some biology lessons somewhat prematurely! I had no idea what all the fuss had been about and it remained a mystery to me for many years.

On Thursday morning, 6th February, 1952 we all lined up for Assembly and Mr Turner had a black armband on his jacket. He solemnly announced that King George VI had died the previous day and that Princess Elizabeth had become Queen Elizabeth II. I started to cry, along with several of the girls – part of my English heritage had gone and it made me so sad. I had listened to the King's Christmas broadcasts for as long as I could remember and I was brought up to have enormous respect for the Royal Family. Princess Elizabeth was on her way to Australia for a Royal Visit when her Father died, and Joanie, Fred, Mum and I were so disappointed that she would not now be coming.

A few days later Joanie and Fred's landlady died. She was 87, and her ailing husband was taken to live with his family in Albury. The house was to be sold and this meant that Joanie and Fred had to move out of the room they rented there. They were both earning good wages by this time, but the search for accommodation met with the same rejections as before ... there was nothing for it, they had to move back into the garage with us. The curtain went up again between the beds and we managed as best we could. It was sort of nice to all be back together again, despite the drawbacks. Joanie and Fred were desperately unhappy in Australia and were saving every penny they could in order to return to England. They didn't talk about their wish to return very much and I think this was because it would mean another parting, but Fred missed his big family so much, he just had to get back to be enveloped in their love, care and concern ... but events were to delay their return for a while.

Chapter 19 – On the move again

After my 11th birthday in March, 1952 I was old enough to 'fly up' to the Girl Guides from the Brownies. I was not popular with the other Guides, but they were unable to refuse me. I didn't have a happy time in the Guides – I was never allowed to go on camp with them and my badges were extraordinarily hard to pass … but I did learn to sing 'Ging Gang Gooly'! The main advantage for me was that I could help Mum with the Brownies, which I really enjoyed. One evening, just as Mum and I were ready in uniform to go to Brownies, there was a knock on the door. Joanie went to see who it was and I heard a joyful scream as she realised it was Peter! There was a bit of a scramble as we all tried to hug and kiss him at once, and it wasn't until we had said our hellos that we realised that he was in an Australian Army uniform. He said he could stay the night, so Mum and I dashed off to Brownies, had what must have been the shortest session in the history of the Brownie movement, and dashed back to the garage. What on earth was Peter doing in the Army? He looked really handsome in his uniform, so Mum got Fred to take a photograph of the three of us together in our uniforms. Then as we sat and ate our meal he explained that because he had been made to leave the 'Big Brother' movement he was no longer exempt from National Service in Australia. He had been called up, and wasn't sure if he would be taken back by the farmer he had worked for at Mulwala at the end of his three months. He was relieved that it was only three months, not two years as in Britain. He was in the middle of his service period and had a 48-hour pass. He apologised to Mum for not letting her know, but his car was taking all his money to keep on the road and he had little left over each week, so paper, envelopes and stamps were not a priority. He didn't like the Army as they were camped in the Dandenong Mountains and it was pretty basic and uncomfortable … but he said he had known worse! We told him about Guy Fawkes Night, which was still imprinted on all our minds – he had to have a little chuckle over our stupidity and he was not in the least bit surprised that we had been chased off.

Mum went up to see if she could borrow the camp bed from Mrs Hornsey, and Peter slept in the living area of the garage on the other side of the curtain. We were all so happy to be together again and the next morning when Peter left he promised to let Mum know what was happening when he was discharged. It was another sad parting, but we hoped that we would see him again soon.

At the beginning of August, Joanie had been chatting to one of the patients at the hospital, an elderly lady called

Miss Gardiner. She had had a nasty fall and was quite frail, but was well enough to return home in the next few days. She asked Joanie if she knew anyone who would be prepared to move into her home in Whitehead Street (but further up from where they had previously lived) and look after her. Joanie came home and discussed it with Fred and he suggested that Joanie find out more. The following day Joanie asked Miss Gardiner for some more details because she might be interested. Miss Gardiner gave the key of her house to Joanie and told her to go with Fred and have a look at it. That evening we all went up to Whitehead Street to have a look. The house was quite old, had been neglected and it was obvious that Miss Gardiner had lived in just one room. There were 4 bedrooms, a big garden, a kitchen, sitting room, and bathroom. The 'dunny' was down at the end of the garden. Because there was no mains drainage most people had a 'dunny' which was a small wooden cubicle with a wooden bench under which was a large can. The 'dunny man' would come once a week, bringing an empty can and a lid, and he would hoist the full can with lid up onto his shoulder and carry it to the truck outside. Where it went to from there I have no idea but it was always nice to have a clean can and, temporarily at least, get rid of the smell. The wooden seat was where red-backed spiders loved to congregate and you had to check under and behind it before using the 'dunny' in case they were there waiting to pounce! We still had cut-up newspaper for toilet paper, hung from a string on the back of the door just like in Camelot Street in London.

When we got back to the garage, there was a long discussion as to what we should all do next. Joanie and

Fred thought that they could manage to take care of Miss Gardiner, but they were also concerned for Mum and me living in the garage. When it rained we had lots of leaks and it was so hot inside when the sun shone. They didn't like the idea of Mum putting up with that sort of accommodation so they asked her if we would come to Whitehead Street with them. Mum thought a lot about it and finally agreed. I was delighted as I was going to have my own bedroom – the first time since we had left London. Joanie asked Miss Gardiner if we could all move in and she seemed very happy at the idea. I think she was a lonely old lady and the prospect of company appealed to her. Once again Mum had to tell Mrs Hornsey that we were moving out, and arrangements were made to move into the house on the day Miss Gardiner was discharged from hospital. Mum and I were introduced to her. She was completely bedridden but she was the sweetest old lady you could imagine. I used to do her shopping for her and she always let me keep the change.

We said a sad farewell to the garage that had been our home for well over a year apart from the month at Mr Maclean's; sometimes it was just Mum and I together, sometimes shared with Joanie and Fred and sometimes even five of us shared it when Peter stayed overnight, but because of the love that Mum brought to the place, because she was determined to make it as comfortable as she could, for me it will always be a place that I will remember as our 'home'.

About a week after we moved in to Whitehead Street, a car pulled up and a gentleman came and let himself in the front door with a key. Fred went through the hall to see what was going on, and asked him what the devil he was doing there. The gentleman asked Fred what **he** was doing there! It turned out to be Miss Gardiner's brother who had come down from Queensland where he owned a pineapple farm, to see if she was out of hospital. He was delighted that his sister was being looked after, but a bit suspicious because we were English. When he learned that Mum, Joanie and Fred all had jobs, I think he was a lot happier, as he obviously thought that we might be going to take advantage of Miss Gardiner. I was a bit upset as I had to move into Mum's room for three nights whilst he stayed, but during that time he was convinced that his sister was being looked after and that the only advantage we had was that we didn't pay any rent. Mum and Joanie would bathe Miss Gardiner, wash and iron her clothes, cook meals (Joanie was an excellent cook!), clean, and I would do the shopping. Fred made himself useful round the house, redecorating and doing the gardening, so the arrangement worked to the benefit of all of us.

Although during this time Joanie and Fred were saving every penny so that they could return to England, Fred managed to buy an old truck, so it was great to have transport when we wanted to get anywhere. Mum had written to Peter giving him our new address but had not received a reply, so Fred suggested that he would take us to Mulwala where Peter had been working before he was called up for National Service to see if we could track him down. We set off one day and when we got near Mulwala we passed a huge lake full of dead trees. The lake had been artificially created and the ghostly bare branches stuck up from the water like a spooky forest, but thousands of sulphur-crested cockatoos were nesting in the trees, looking like so many Christmas decorations gleaming in the sun. I thought it was an enchanting place!

We found the farm that Peter had been working at with Sid and went to the farmhouse to enquire whether they were still there. We were told that they were out somewhere on the farm working – when we explained who we were we were directed to the shearers' quarters and told that we could wait there. It wasn't too long before we heard voices outside the quarters and a group of men filed in, looking tired and dusty. They looked astonished to see us and were about to demand what we were doing there – the last two in were Peter and Sid and there was another mad rush to hug and kiss Peter. We were introduced to all the men, including Sid, who turned out to be a good-looking young man, not as tall as Peter, but just as tanned and healthy looking. I liked him straight away. Peter was surprised that Fred had been able to afford a truck and I think he was a little envious because Peter had had to sell his beloved little Triumph Mayflower – the pay in the Army had been so bad he was unable to afford the car, but he was grateful to the farmer for taking him back. It was truly wonderful to catch up with Peter again and once they had cleaned up the men cooked a meal of eggs and baked beans which they invited us to share with them.

As we were about to leave I saw Joanie and Fred having a conspiratorial whisper with Peter, and Mum standing nearby with a big grin on her face. Suddenly Peter lifted Joanie into his arms and off her feet shouting "Hurray, I'm going to be an Uncle!". It took me a few seconds to work out the implications of this and then I realised that

Joanie must be expecting a baby! Why hadn't anyone told me? Mum explained that the purpose of the trip to see Peter was for us all to be together when Joanie made it public. I was so excited ... I was going to be an Aunty! The other men all shook Fred's hand and gave Joanie a congratulatory kiss. It was hard to leave Peter again and without transport there was no way that he would be able to visit us, but at least he had our new address so he promised to keep in touch. On the way home I was full of questions – when was the baby coming, would it be a girl or boy, what were they going to call it? The adults laughed at my eagerness to know all the facts – Mum had never told me the facts of life so it all seemed like magic to me. Looking back, I realise that when we all lived in the garage, the nights that Mum and I took the Brownie group must have been heaven for Joanie and Fred, the only chance they ever really got to be on their own ... but I didn't know that then!

About a month later I arrived home from school and was surprised to see two big motorbikes in the drive. I thought that they might perhaps belong to some of Fred's friends from the hospital, but when I went round the back there on the steps sat Peter and Sid. My heart leapt with joy ... here was my lovely brother and his gorgeous friend! We waited until Mum, Joanie and Fred came home from work and then they told us all that Sid had become really disillusioned at the way he was being treated as a 'Little Brother' and had decided to branch out on his own with Peter. They had both saved up enough money to buy motorbikes and planned to travel round Australia doing seasonal work and seeing the country. They slept on the lounge floor that night and left early the next morning.

Before they left Sid gave me a present of a beautiful bible which I still have to this day. I was sad to see them go, but I was confident that we would see them again eventually so I consoled myself with that fact.

Mum was happy working at Maples and we babysat a lot for the Rippingales. Joanie and Fred had also started babysitting, and between the four of us we managed to keep the Lethbridges, the Fergusons, and the Rippingales happy. Joanie and Fred continued to work at the hospital and they continued to save. Joanie got larger and larger as the weeks went by and she would let me feel the baby kicking by putting a gentle hand on her tummy. She was convinced that she was going to have a footballer! Joanie got some strange cravings too … she told Fred that she wanted some cockles, indeed, **must** have some. Poor Fred – miles from any sea and no fishmonger in town – what was he to do? One Saturday morning we all got up early and caught the train to Melbourne. When we arrived we headed for the sea front and there at last Fred found a fishmonger who had cockles. Joanie devoured them, she couldn't get enough! We had a paddle in the sea and then we all caught the tram to Luna Park, the funfair that we had visited with the girls from our cabin on the SS Orion. Joanie was unable to go on the roller-coaster so we all watched as the people sat in the little trains and screamed as the roller-coaster rushed around. I had a candy-floss, the first one ever, but ended up sticky from head to foot! It was magical to me and at the end of the day when we caught the train back I thought it had been the very best day that we had spent in Australia ever. Fred brought a bag of cockles back and Joanie ate them the next day, then she had to manage without them, but she eventually decided that she wanted peanut butter all the time and that was much easier to come by!

Opposite us in Whitehead Street lived a boy that I had noticed coming in and out of his house, sometimes on foot, sometimes on his bike. He was tall, handsome, and a couple of years older than me. I started to get a crush on him and would spend hours in the front garden so that when he left his house I could smile at him and see his lovely smile back. His name was Tony Crisp and I idolised him. I was still only 11, but every time I went to the pictures, the children all used to sit at the front in the Rex Cinema and I was longing for him to sit next to me. I think he was practically oblivious to my existence and he always had an older girl to sit next to. I would sit with Brenda and sometimes the Hornseys, but my attention always strayed elsewhere. Besides, I had seen all the Roy Rogers, Batman and Superman films in London at the ABC Cinema so I didn't have to concentrate!

A lady stopped Mum in the street one day and said *"I'm so sorry to hear about your son, Mrs Baker"*. Mum asked her what she meant, and the reply just devastated Mum. She said *"I heard he was killed in a motorcycle accident"*. Mum collapsed in the street, and the lady helped Mum up, and told her that she had heard that the accident had been at Goulburn. Mum was sobbing and frantic, and didn't know what to do, so she went to the Police Station and asked if they could contact the Police at Goulburn and find out what had happened. The Police were very offhand and not at all concerned about Mum's plight, but eventually were able to ascertain that Peter **had** been involved in an accident and he had been injured, but certainly not killed. The shock took its toll on Mum, she was shaking and ashen, and she was unable to work any more that day. Mr Rippingale got in touch with the hospital and Fred came in the truck to pick her up and take her back to Whitehead Street, There then happened the greatest irony that I have ever come across – when they arrived at the house, there in the letter-box was a letter from Peter, dated two weeks previously, saying he had been hit by a car at a crossroad, and although his motorcycle was badly damaged he had only suffered a broken arm and cuts and bruises. He and Sid were going to stay in the area until his arm was better and the motorcycle repaired, and she was not to worry. Poor Mum! She had been through one of the worst days of her life, and all for nothing. Peter's letter certainly eased her mind, but it just demonstrated how news that is passed from pillar to post can become distorted in the process.

I came home from school a couple of weeks later to see a motorcycle outside the house – I did not need three guesses this time, and I ran inside and leapt into Peter's arms. Peter had called at Maples to see Mum – she was so relieved to see that he was OK, and she gave him the keys to the house and asked him to make Miss Gardiner a cup of tea and wait for us all to get home. I asked him where Sid was, and he told me to be patient and I would find out. When Mum, Joanie and Fred arrived home from work they made some sandwiches and we sat in the kitchen as Peter unfolded a strange story. When he and Sid had reached Sydney they were very short of money and unable to find any work. They were getting desperate so Sid suggested that they **burgle** a house. Peter was horrified and refused point-blank. The next morning Sid had disappeared, taking the small amount of money which was all that Peter had left, and none of us ever saw him again. I still treasured the Bible he had given me but I felt so let down by him. Fortunately Peter kept his watch on at night, so he had had to pawn that to get enough money to find his way back to Corowa. Mum immediately said that he could stay with us – I was so pleased – so she made him up a bed in the sleep-out and we were both thrilled to have him with us. A few days later Mrs Maclean told Mum that she had room for a lodger, so Peter moved into her house in Tower Street.

Peter managed to find a job at Lindemans, a local vineyard – sometimes I would ride pillion on his motorbike to where he worked and we would pick some small, sweet sultana grapes and take them home. There were no motorcycle helmet rules in those days so we were completely unprotected, and we would race along the dirt roads at what seemed like 100 miles an hour, me clinging on round his waist for dear life!

After a while Peter changed jobs – he was fed up with the work at the vineyard, and he managed to get a job as Trainee Electrician with Hook's, a furniture and electrical shop in Sanger Street. Graham and Norma Hook had two young sons, Peter and Michael … and it wasn't long before Mum and I were babysitting for the Hooks, too. They were a lovely family, and treated us well. Peter quickly learned the trade and was an asset to them, often travelling many miles to deliver furniture, repair customer's electrical goods, or occasionally install air conditioning in customers' houses – in those days, this was a very new concept, and very expensive.

The Hooks were friendly with a couple who owned the nurseries in Corowa, and they mentioned to Mum that their friends needed someone to pot up plants and generally do odd jobs around the place. They wondered whether I might be interested in the job, so Mum took me for an interview with Mr Figgins and I got the job, so I worked there at the weekends and after school. I didn't get paid very much, but I just loved potting up the plants, particularly the 'sensitive mimosa', which at the slightest touch, or even a shaking of the pot, would fold its leaves down, looking for all the world as if it were dead. The gardener explained that the plants originally grew in the desert and as the ground vibrated from the footsteps of the camels the plant pretended to die to prevent being eaten. The nursery specialised in chrysanthemums, and I was often allowed to take some flowers home for Mum.

Before school broke up for the long summer holiday I had been given a form to take home to select which subjects I wanted to do at High School, where I would start in January the following year. Most of the children moved up from Primary School to High School at 11 years old, but if there were children who could not keep up with the top class in Primary School they were made to repeat the last year of Primary School. This created a strange mix of children in any one class, some being a year older than their classmates and usually they progressed all the way through High School in a lower class than their age warranted. If they improved there was always the opportunity for them to move up a class, but sometimes they fell behind again and were moved back down. Although I hadn't been in England to take my 11-plus, it always seemed to me to be a much better way of sorting out the more clever ones from the less gifted! Anyway, when Mum saw the form that she had to fill out she noticed that there was a choice between French, Science and Business Principles, or Domestic Science which included cookery. Realizing that her cookery skills were sadly lacking, she decided that I would learn to cook properly so she enrolled me in the Domestic Science stream and I returned the paper to school. I don't think Mr Turner could have cared less what I chose to do and the form was sent to the High School with all the others.

Chapter 20 – A New Arrival!

We celebrated Christmas in Miss Gardiner's house and she joined in the celebrations with us. Fred carried her gently from her bedroom in the lounge and we had a roast chicken with all the trimmings – we just did not have the heart to go for a picnic and leave Miss Gardiner on her own, but it was **so** hot cooking in the house in the blistering heat of an Australian summer. Poor Joanie was suffering with the heat, and so was Mum. I had got myself badly sunburned and had huge water blisters on my shoulders which Mum burst with a needle. These blisters turned septic and I could hardly bear my shoulders to be touched. Some nights I would lie on the linoleum floor to try to cool myself down, but there was no respite. We never realised the damage that we were doing to our skin by not protecting it, but I seemed to suffer the most.

There was a big clump of oleander in the front garden and I managed to make a 'den' in the middle of it where I would sit for hours reading. Years later Brenda told me that an old bushman wanted something to stir his tea with, so he broke a piece from an oleander bush and used that – he died shortly afterwards, so poisonous was the sap of the bush. When I think of the number of times that I must have got sap on my hands from wriggling into my 'den', I think I am lucky to be alive – and I am thankful that I stopped biting my nails at an early age!

On Saturday, 17th January, 1953 Mum and I babysat for the Hooks. Just before Mr and Mrs Hook left for their evening out, Mum asked if she could take a photograph of the family in front of their car. It was a happy family group, but Mum could not have possibly realised the significance of this photograph at the time. The next day the Hooks went to Corowa Common for a picnic by the river, and during the afternoon little Peter, aged six and a half, disappeared. Practically the whole town joined the search which went on for days, but sadly his body was never found. There were theories about him being kidnapped – the thorough search left no stone unturned, even to the point of dynamiting huge logs under the surface of the river in case the body was trapped there, with no success. The Hook family was distraught, and it was only after some time that Mum was able to give them a copy of the photograph she had taken when we babysat – the last one ever taken of little Peter. It was the first time that I had felt so close to a tragedy, and I was very traumatised by it. I had grown very fond of the two little boys, and found it hard to understand why such cruel things happened to such nice people.

In late January, 1953 I started at the High School along with Brenda, Maureen, Dawn, Gloria and most of the other children from my class. I was so proud to be there, and now I was allowed to ride my bicycle to school. The problem with that was that there were a whole new set of children who thought it was hilarious to see a girl on a boy's bike, so I suffered more taunts, but I think my skin was getting tougher because I just poked my tongue out at them and ignored the insults.

During the first couple of weeks I had the lessons that we all had to do – Mathematics, English Language, English Literature, Geography, History, and also at the appointed times I would join the Cookery and Domestic Science lessons. One day I was summoned into the Headmaster's Office – I was petrified, not knowing what I had done wrong. The Headmaster, Mr Bryan, was a strict disciplinarian and one did not dare put a foot wrong in his presence. He asked me why I had selected Domestic Science as my preferred stream and I told him that Mum was keen for me to learn to cook. "*Tell her to come to see me at 1pm tomorrow! Dismiss!*". I scuttled out from his office, and after school I rode up to Maples and went in to see Mum. I told her what Mr Bryan had said and she asked if she could have her lunch break at 1pm the next day. Mr Rippingale agreed, and so the next day I stood trembling outside Mr Bryan's office with Mum. I was told to wait outside. I was convinced I had done something so bad they would probably execute me! When Mum came out she had a serious look on her face. I daren't ask her what I had done so we walked up to the Victoria Gardens in silence. Once we were sat on a park bench she told me that the teachers who taught Mathematics, English Language, Geography and History were all disappointed that I had opted to take Domestic Science as I was more than capable of taking French, Science and Business Principles. Mr Bryan had therefore decided that I should change streams straight away. Mum, bless her, thought that this would be a retrograde step for me as I would never be able to cook! It turned out to be a choice for which I was ever grateful to Mr Bryan as it gave me the opportunity of some good academic qualifications at a later date ... and I also learned to cook well later on, too!

Little did I realise the impact this change would have on my class mates. The ones who were doing Domestic Science wouldn't speak to me because I had been highlighted as having more academic potential than them, and the ones I joined in French, Science and Business Principles hated me because I had been specifically selected to join a more academic group than they felt I warranted. Fortunately for me the lovely, loyal Brenda remained at my side as a true and supportive friend. Our teachers were Mr Weir, Miss Kerr, Mr Tyrrell and Mr LeSage. Mr LeSage taught Mathematics, but was not very good looking, and Mr Tyrrell taught French, and was very handsome. However, although the girls all worshipped him at first we were soon to learn that he had a foul temper, and he would throw the wooden blackboard cleaner at you with surprising accuracy if he thought that you weren't paying attention. Mr LeSage and I got on famously because I was good at Mathematics, and when he started up a photographic club after school he taught us pupils all the rudiments of photography from taking photos to printing and developing them. I idolised him, he was an excellent teacher. Mr Weir taught Art and Business Principles, and Miss Kerr taught Geography. They were a pair of lovebirds, always holding hands when they thought that they were out of sight, and they eventually married. I got on well with both of them and enjoyed their lessons.

I also enjoyed gymnastics and games, but I rarely got selected to play in any of the school teams. I wasn't even allowed to join the hockey class but looking back, I am not too disappointed at that. The girls who played always seemed to have great bruises on their legs and ankles. I was fairly good at tennis and very good at basketball, but was usually the spectator when it came to playing other teams. On one occasion our year performed a gymnastic display for visitors and parents, but again I was not selected to be part of the display. However, I enjoyed Friday afternoon sports, but occasionally used the excuse that my leg injury hurt when I wanted to revise for an exam or go home early!

I was still working at the nursery, and when the High School had a flower festival I was able to provide 300 chrysanthemum heads, generously donated by Mr Figgins. This increased my popularity with the organisers of the festival, but did nothing to improve my popularity with the pupils.

Part of our curriculum included ballroom dancing, and I had noticed Graeme Phipps in our class and developed a crush on him. He was very good looking and had wonderful curly hair. We were made to dance with the boys and I just used to tremble when I danced with him, as a result of which he preferred not to dance with me. Never mind, I learned the steps better with any of the other boys as I could concentrate more! I was nearly 12, and on one of the times when we went to the cinema I sat at the front with the other children when, to my surprise, Graeme came up and asked if he could sit with me. I was overjoyed and couldn't wait to tell Mum. She smiled and said "*Watch what he gets up to!*", but I had no idea what she meant. After three or four times of sitting holding hands with him in the cinema he changed allegiance and preferred someone else, so I suffered a very juvenile broken heart!

Mum had a great sense of humour and if she heard a joke she liked, she would write it down in a book in shorthand so that I was unable to read what was probably some very risqué material! She also collected rude jokes and drawings on paper and she kept these all in a box together. One night we were all sitting talking after tea and Mum got her box of jokes out. One of them was a short play about a couple who were trying for a baby without success, and they had been told by the Government that they would have to send a man round from the 'Ministry of Population' to 'assist'. On the appointed day the husband went to work and a knock came on the door. The wife, who was very nervous, assumed it was the man from the 'Ministry', but in actual fact it was a door-to-door photographer. The wife asked him in and asked him about his work, to which he replied, amongst other things, that he liked to work in the park because it was a more natural setting, but the squirrels kept nibbling his equipment, and that he had tried once on the top of a bus, but he got so bounced around that he lost his concentration. We were all laughing so much and although I didn't appreciate all the '*double-entendres*', I thought it was hilarious. I asked Mum if I could take it to school and she said it was OK as long as I didn't let the teachers see it. In class I sat next to a boy called Earl Ryan and I told him about the joke that I had in my pocket.

He asked to see it so I told him he could at break-time, but he pestered me until I surreptitiously got it out of my pocket and handed it to him ... and he promptly dropped it! Mr Weir, our teacher, missed nothing and so he asked Earl to give him what must be a 'very important piece of paper to be reading it in the lesson'. I went puce as Earl told Mr Weir that it was my paper – Mr Weir opened it up, read the first page and with a face like thunder he told me to leave the class. Once again I was hauled up in front of Mr Bryan, who read the play and then asked me if I had read it. I told him the truth, so he sat me in the corridor and made me write the whole play out from memory. The other children were curious as to what I was writing but I said nothing, although Earl told them it was a rude joke. I went home that afternoon with a stern letter from Mr Bryan saying that if ever I brought 'filth' like that to school again I would be expelled. Mum said it was my own fault, I should have been more sensible – and I never again got to see anything from the box!

I used to meet Mum in the Victoria Gardens for lunch each school day. We sat on a park bench and one day I stretched my right arm out behind Mum along the back of the bench. When I brought my arm back I was surprised to see that the vein running up the inside of my arm had turned a bright red colour. I had not felt a bite at all but we assumed that it must be one. Mum couldn't afford to pay to go to the Doctor's so she told me to go to see the teacher when I returned to school after lunch. This I did, and Miss Kerr was very worried and took me to the first aid room to put some cream on it. She told me to keep an eye on it and if it got any worse to let her know. During the afternoon my arm swelled up, so I put my hand up to ask Mr Tyrrell if I could go to Miss Kerr as instructed. He refused to let me leave his class, so I had to wait until the bell went. Fortunately by this time the swelling had started to reduce, so when I finally got to see Miss Kerr she said that it didn't look any worse and told me to get back to my class. By the time lessons were over for the afternoon the red vein had become pink and I felt no more ill-effects. I can only assume it was a spider bite and was glad that it wasn't a red-backed spider or I might not have been here to tell the tale!

There was great excitement at the Church, as Canon Ross-Edwards was due to retire, and the Ordination of the new Rector, Canon David Wicking, was going to take place. Everyone was sad to see Canon Ross-Edwards leave. He had been so very kind to us at a time when we needed help desperately and he was truly grateful to Mum for starting the Brownie pack. Many years later his family had a stained glass window installed in St John's Church to his memory. The Ordination Service was very moving and Canon Wicking settled into his new post. I had started Confirmation Classes, so I got to know him fairly well, and he was respected by everyone.

My 12th birthday arrived and as it was a Friday I went to school as usual. Joanie was by this time quite heavy with her pregnancy and was not working. That evening we had a celebratory meal – Miss Gardiner was carried through from her bedroom to join in the celebrations, so it was a real party.

Early in April, Joanie began to get pains, and on 5th April, 1953 she went into labour. Normally, if you had a baby in Corowa Hospital, the charges were very expensive but because Joanie worked there she was able to have her delivery free. On 6th April she produced the most beautiful baby girl, Denise, and I was allowed to visit her and see the baby, although normally children were not allowed to visit in the Maternity Ward. Fred looked like he had won a million pounds, so proud was he of his new daughter. Joanie returned to Whitehead Street from hospital and Miss Gardiner was delighted to welcome this new arrival into her establishment. Sadly, Miss Gardiner was getting very frail, but the new baby in the house seemed to give her a new lease of life. Denise was indeed a treasure, she was a contented, happy baby full of smiles and chuckles and she brought a kind of peace to a world that was difficult for us all.

Chapter 21 – On the move yet again!

I had enjoyed the Confirmation classes with the new Rector, Canon David Wicking, and on 30th April, 1953 I was confirmed by the Bishop of Riverina, Bishop Robinson, along with 33 other children and adults in St John's Church. Mum bought me a white skirt for the Confirmation service which I wore with a white school blouse and that proved to be perfect for the ceremony. She was able to borrow a veil embroidered with a cross from the Church, and she bought me some white shoes and gloves – I will remember the Service forever, it was so solemn and holy. After I was Confirmed I took Holy Communion with Mum every Sunday.

Mum was reading the '*Corowa Free Press*' when she noticed that Coreen Shire Council needed a Secretary. She enjoyed her job at Maples, but yearned to be able to use her secretarial skills more so she applied for the job, expecting to be told 'get lost' or something less polite. Mr Tasker, the Town Clerk, interviewed her and she was most surprised to be given the job. It meant more money so she was delighted.

Mr Tasker was a portly, quite stern man with one leg shorter than the other, so he wore a boot with three or four inches of sole and heel to compensate. He still walked with a rolling gait and I found him quite intimidating, but Mum did her job well so he respected her, but never made much of an effort to be friendly towards her. There were two other people in the office – Winsley Howard, who was one of Brenda's cousins and a middle-aged lady called Miss Edna Dawe.

Winsley was beautiful. She dressed like a beauty queen and had long dark hair that she wore in plaits wrapped round her head. I thought she was the loveliest person in Corowa. Winsley invited us to her house to meet her family. She was the eldest of seven children – Coral, Richard, Margaret, Winston, Jeanie and Andrew were her siblings. Her Father, who I called Uncle Duff, was the English brother of Brenda's Father. Her Mother, Aunty Cora, was the sweetest, most patient and most generous lady that I have ever come across. They lived in a lovely big house which Uncle Duff had built, and added to as the family increased in size. Most noticeable at the front of the house was a big white concrete swan which was nearly always filled with flowers tumbling out of it down the front porch wall. Winsley could play the piano and I often used to go and sit next to her on the piano stool in the front parlour whilst she played all sorts of classical pieces including '*Für Elise*', which was my favourite. Uncle Duff often used to take us all to Lake Moodemere where we would sail in the small sailing boat called 'Ripple' that he had built.

About a month after Mum started working for Coreen Shire Council she heard that a 'council house' in King Street, way out on the outskirts of Corowa past the Showground, had become vacant and was due to be demolished. Mum asked Mr Tasker if there was any chance of her renting it. She, and Joanie and Fred, had become increasingly worried about Miss Gardiner, who was obviously nearing the end of her life, so she was keen to find somewhere else to live. Although reluctant, Mr Tasker gave Mum the key to go and have a look. That evening, Mum, Fred and I went up to King Street in Fred's truck – Pash and me sitting on the flat bed at the back – and as we pulled up our hearts sank. The house was very typical, built of horizontal boards with a corrugated iron roof which was very rusty. It stood in quite a large garden with a lawn at the front and two large peppercorn trees on the left-hand side. It had a driveway on the right-hand side which led down to the back garden where there were some fruit trees and at the very far end of which was the 'dunny'. The tall corrugated iron fence across the end of the garden divided us from the Showground. There was another similar house next door, and five children stood curiously in their garden, watching our every move. On the other side was the council yard where they kept all their heavy equipment, reels of wire and various other bits and pieces, but fortunately the peppercorn trees screened us from this eyesore. The house had a run-down, neglected look and the garden was badly in need of some attention.

Mum unlocked the front door which opened into a lounge with a large bedroom on the left and a smaller one further down on the left. From the smaller bedroom you gained access to the 'sleepout', a veranda enclosed by fly-netting. A door at the far end of the lounge led through into a strange area. From this area a door led into a kitchen with a bathroom leading off at the right-hand end. It was obvious that at one time the kitchen and bathroom area had been a completely separate building to the front of the house, and the strange area in between had been created by someone filling the ends with packing case material (just as I had seen in Aden!), using more packing case material as the floor, and completing the structure with a corrugated iron roof that was rusting and had small holes where daylight shone through. We immediately christened this area 'the place you walk through' because that's about all you could do with it. This name stuck and we called it that until we moved out. When it rained the water poured through the roof of 'the place you walk through', so we had to keep an umbrella in the lounge and another one in the kitchen so that we could get through from one side to the other without getting drenched! We also kept a variety of buckets and bowls in there to catch the water where the roof leaked. The whole place was in shocking decorative order, inside and out, but again Mum, with her spirit unbowed by the taunts and insults of the past two years, was able to visualise this place as home. I was not too keen as there were cobwebs everywhere, but Fred told Mum that if she took it on he and Joanie would help us clean it up.

Mum told Mr Tasker that she would like to rent it, so he shrugged his shoulders and told her that she could have it for ten shillings a week – Mum thought this was a bargain considering it was what she had paid for just a garage! From then on we spent all our spare time scrubbing, cleaning, painting and gardening until the place looked half-decent. Joanie and Fred insisted on staying with Miss Gardiner to the end – none of us would have allowed her to be abandoned, so the arrangement worked out well. Mum and I had a house to ourselves, and Joanie and Fred had almost all of Miss Gardiner's house to themselves, so Denise was able to have a cot in a room on her own. It was a long bike ride into school and work every day but it was great to have all that space to ourselves. We stored the sea-chest and the cases in 'the place you walk through'. Mum had the large bedroom and I had the small one. Mr Rippingale at Maples was kind to Mum, giving her a small discount as an ex-employee on the things she had to buy. We still babysat for the Rippingales, the Lethbridges and the Fergusons on a regular basis and I occasionally babysat Denise when Mum, Joanie and Fred went to the pictures to see a horror film … after 'Unknown Island' I was not keen to see anything else that frightened me so!

One night I heard strange noises in my bedroom and it scared me, so I went into Mum's room to see if she could find out what it was. We both stood in my room and heard the strangest grunting noises, but although we searched we could find nothing. I was too frightened to sleep in my own room so I spent the rest of the night cuddling up to Mum. The next day at work Mum mentioned the noises and her work colleagues laughed so much. They told her that it was most likely to be possums, animals about the size of a cat with a long striped tail which get between the two layers of wall and make grunting noises. Once I knew that they were harmless I didn't mind so much, but some nights they kept me awake for ages. I also had a bat in my room on one occasion but that made its own way out and thankfully didn't re-appear.

In the garden stood a pipe with a long handle on the top which moved with an upside-down pendulum effect. We found out after we moved in that this was the pump for the cesspit where all the waste water from the sink and the bath went to, and it had to be pumped out once a week onto the garden. It was back-breaking and arm-breaking work, and it became my job exclusively because Mum was not strong enough to work the pump, which had to be primed with clean water to get it going and pumped for about an hour to empty all the water out. It smelled foul and was the worst job I had undertaken so far – even worse than chopping chooks heads off! Nothing would grow where the water lay on the garden, so that side was unused. On the other side we tried to grow vegetables but it was a constant struggle to keep the blistering sun from shrivelling them up. In the winter we had 'black frosts' which killed everything and turned all the grass black, and it was so cold cycling to school that my fingers froze to the metal handlebars of my old bicycle.

At the end of the back garden was an old chook pen, so Mum decided to keep some chooks to have fresh eggs. She talked to one of the farmers that came into the Council Office to pay his rates, and he sold her a dozen young chicks. We noticed after a couple of weeks that they were losing their feathers and we weren't sure if this was normal or not, so we asked the neighbours. Mr Poidevin came round, took one look at them, and said "*They're covered in ticks*". He told us that we had to paint sump oil on all the wood of the pen and disinfect it before we kept any more chooks. He also said that this must be done on a regular basis to keep the pen tick-free. Mum was able to obtain some sump oil from the council yard next door to us and I painted all the wood – it was a horrible job and I got covered in sump oil from head to foot ... and this had to be done once a month! We disinfected everything and got some more chicks ... we soon had a pen full of healthy chickens that were good layers. Mum decided to get a rooster and so eventually we were able to produce our own chicks ... enough to lay plenty of eggs and also to use for food.

We had problems with rats killing our chooks so Mum eventually acquired four cats – Sooty, Sammy, Snuffy and Snowy. It was quite a mouthful when you had to call them in for their food, but they were good ratters so we had resolved that problem. We had by this time also managed to accumulate several birds ... a sulphur-crested cockatoo, some budgerigars, a Mountain Lowrie and a galah. So with our chooks, parrots, cats and Pash we had quite a menagerie.

Another problem we had was that there was a huge nest of meat ants in the back garden. These ants were about a half an inch long, and if we were working in the garden they would run up our legs and bite us ... and boy, did they hurt! We were advised to pour boiling water into the entrances to the nest, and this worked temporarily, but they soon came back, so one day when I was painting the chook pen with sump oil, I had some left over and I decided to pour that down into the nest. It worked! They were very tenacious, but it was ages before they came back, and each time I used the sump oil to good effect.

Mr and Mrs Poidevin were friendly neighbours, were good to us when it came to advice, but there was no practical help from them at all. We never asked for, nor expected, any help but I do believe that had a woman in her 50's with a young child been in a similar situation in England the post-war community spirit would have prevailed. I used to play with three of the children – Ivan, Harry and Leonie. We would go for bike rides to Almond Lane, which was a row of almond trees some distance out of the town, where we would pick the almonds and sit and eat a lot before taking the remainder back home. We would also ride out on Honour Avenue to Mulberry Farm where there was a huge cactus where we carved our names.

In the bathroom in the house in King Street was a chip heater, which heated the water by means of lighting a fire inside the heater and feeding it with wood chips. There were plenty of wood chips available as I used to chop lots of wood for the fire in the lounge, which we used in the bitter cold of the winter. The trouble was, if you fed too many chips into the heater the hot water coming out of the spout into the bath had a mind of its own – it used to spurt out spasmodically and you could find yourself marooned up one end of the bath trying to avoid getting scalded. All you could do was shout for someone to come in and throw water on the fire to prevent the whole thing from blowing up ... but at least it was nice to be able to have a bath!

The Hooks had decided to leave Corowa, so Peter was without a job. He left Mrs MacLean's and came to live with us, using the 'sleep-out' as his room. He soon found more work with an electrical company, and it was good to have a man in the house ... at least there was someone there to empty the cesspit!

In the summer it got so hot that we all had to sleep in the lounge on the linoleum floor to keep cool. As we couldn't afford to buy a refrigerator Mum bought an 'ice chest', an early form of refrigerator. There was a lid that opened upwards into a large, metal-lined compartment, and into this you put a huge block of ice, which gradually melted but kept the food cool in the lower compartment. You had to catch the melted water in a bucket underneath which constantly had to be emptied, and many were the times I came home from school and there would be a puddle under the ice chest where the bucket had overflowed. We also had a problem obtaining the blocks of ice. The ice supplier refused to deliver to us – "*we don't deliver to bloody pommies*" – so Fred used to bring us a block whenever we needed one, but by the time he reached the house, a lot of the block had already melted. This meant that we had to buy them more frequently than most people. Eventually Mum was able to afford an electric refrigerator, and it was a great relief not to have to keep an eye on the melting ice.

Mum decided that she would treat us all to a coach trip to Mt Buffalo where we would be able to see snow. Mrs Hornsey agreed to babysit Denise, so we got up early, dropped Denise off in Walker Street and then caught the coach, which took us through some beautiful scenery to the mountain. When we arrived we revelled in the snow, we had all missed it so much – we had snowball fights and built a snowman. I think that seeing the snow made

Fred even more homesick, but he joined in the fun with us and we all enjoyed the day. It was strange to think that there were people on that coach who had never seen snow and were taking the trip especially to do so.

Sadly, Miss Gardiner died and the house was sold, so Joanie, Fred and Denise had to find somewhere else to live. Although the plan had been to have Joanie and Fred living with us in the sleepout when this happened, we now had Peter using that as his room. Joanie had become quite friendly with Mrs Hornsey's Mother, Mrs Wright (Granny Wright), when we lived at the garage, and she provided the solution – she was at home all day, so Joanie and Fred could live with her. Joanie could go back to work and she would babysit Denise. Joanie and Fred were keen on this idea as they were saving hard to return to England. Fred was desperately unhappy in Australia and missed his family very much. Granny Wright was lovely and I used to visit her house to see Joanie and Fred often. Denise was growing into a most beautiful baby and I was allowed to take her out for walks in the pram after school. They lived at the bottom of quite a steep hill in Corowa and one Friday I was cycling down this hill to visit them after school and thought I would be clever and take my feet off the pedals. Being a fixed-wheel bike the pedals went round more and more quickly until the poor old bicycle could stand the strain no longer and the chain snapped. It snaked up and hit one of my legs, cutting me quite badly, and I ended up falling off the bike into a patch of stinging nettles. Several of the school children cycled past me, laughing and shouting "Look at 'Gun-daggy' in the nettles!", but not one of them stopped to help me. I limped down to Granny Wright's house, where she cleaned my cuts and grazes, and put witch hazel on the stings. When Joanie and Fred came home from work, Fred ran me and my bike back home and Peter repaired it for me.

When Peter visited the Council Offices to see Mum, the lovely Winsley did not go un-noticed, and for a time we thought that he and Winsley might end up together, but it was not to be. Peter then started courting Babs Rolton, the aunt of a girl at school called Joyce. Joyce had not been friendly towards me until Peter and Babs got engaged, but then we used to visit the Rolton family quite often and Joyce and I became friends. They lived near the airport, and Mum and I would cycle out there sometimes. One day we left our bikes leaning up against the front fence, and when we came out Mum did not notice that a brown snake had wound itself into the spokes on her back wheel. We set off, me behind Mum, and I called to her to stop as she had a stick or something caught in her wheel. When she stopped and saw what it was she threw her bicycle on the ground and we retreated to a safe distance. The snake was none the worse for his experience but he was not about to leave the bicycle, and Mum was not about to ride it again, so we had to leave the bike there and walk home, me pushing my bike, to get Peter to come and sort the snake out. I went with him on the back of his motorbike, and when he saw what sort of snake it was he was horrified. Brown snakes are one of the most venomous, so Mum had had a lucky escape. Peter managed to dislodge the snake which slithered off into the brown grass, completely camouflaged. I rode Mum's bicycle home, constantly looking behind me at the rear wheel in case the snake had decided to catch us up!

The Roltons had some relatives who ran a eucalyptus farm near Bendigo, and they invited us to go there for a holiday. Joyce Rolton, Mum and I caught the train to Bendigo in the school holidays and Les and Eric, the two sons of the farmer, picked us up at the station. They had a lovely house right in the bush and from the first day Joyce, Mum and I helped with the harvesting. The branches were cut from small eucalyptus trees and transported back to the farm on the back of a truck. Joyce and I sat on top of the load, and when we reached the farm the branches had to be unloaded into a huge circular vat. The branches were packed down, a lid was screwed tightly down over them, and then a fire was lit underneath a water container below the vat to create steam, which filtered up through the branches. The steam then burst the tiny bubbles of eucalyptus in the leaves, and the eucalyptus oil ran out through a funnel at the base of the vat and was collected in a bottle. The process was long and laborious, and each load only produced about a couple of pints of oil. When the process was over the lid was lifted to allow the remains of the branches to cool down, then we had to pitchfork them out and start all over again.

Whilst we were there, Eric and Les took us to a disused gold mine, where we were lowered down into the mine by a rope on a winch. It was dark and scary down there, and we had to crawl on all fours, using torches to see our way. Mum found a small gold nugget along one of the passages and I found a beautiful quartz crystal. We were sad when the holiday was over; we had had such an interesting time there.

Chapter 22 – Another Sad Parting

As the winter of 1953 gradually turned into spring, Joanie and Fred had almost saved up enough money to return to England. They booked their passage home for the beginning of December, 1953 on the SS Orontes (20,000 tons), another Orient Line ship, but they also decided that they wanted to visit Sydney before they left as they would never get another chance. Peter was due to go away for two weeks holiday to the north of Australia on his motorbike, so it was arranged that Joanie and Fred would move into the sleepout for their final two weeks, and they would go to Sydney whilst we babysat Denise.

Joanie and Fred had a wonderful four days in Sydney, and Mum and I just loved looking after Denise. Mum knew that she would miss her lovely grand-daughter so much, so she revelled in being able to have her (almost!) to herself. I had lots of cuddles with Denise, too, as I knew that Mum would not be the only one to miss her. Joanie and Fred returned from Sydney and started the final preparation for their long journey back to England. They still only had their clothes and personal effects as they had not really accumulated any furniture or other large items. Joanie's bicycle was carefully wrapped in brown paper ready for transportation. Fred sold his truck, and their cases were packed.

Whilst Joanie and Fred were staying with us a circus arrived in Corowa and set up the Big Top on the Showground, just beyond our back boundary. One of the circus acts was a lion-tamer and the cages with the lions in were parked right up against the other side of our back fence. Their roars could be heard all the time and at night it was particularly scary. The first night we all lay in our respective rooms listening to the roars, when Fred shouted out to me "*Joanie and I will be OK, Titch, because lions go for the young meat first!*". As the only access to the sleepout was through my bedroom I could see what he meant. I did, of course, have a completely sleepless night, hiding under my bedclothes and wondering whether I was going to provide a tasty meal for an escaped lion or not!

Two days before they were due to sail Peter returned from holiday. He had really enjoyed it, except that he had been invited on an 'Abo-shoot' by some Australian men he met and was horrified to find that, even in the 1950's, it was still considered a sport to hunt down and shoot Aboriginal men, rape their females, and take the children as slaves. He apparently told the men what he thought of their invitation and was rewarded with a beating. We were all sickened by this news – Joanie and Fred were even more glad to be leaving, and Mum and I began to think we had been let off lightly in terms of the discrimination that we had experienced.

The day before they were due to sail we all got up early ready to catch the train to Melbourne. Joanie took me in her arms and cuddled me, and told me to look after Mum. Then she said she had a parting present for me, and she took me into 'the place you walk through'. The cases were on the front porch but her bicycle was still wrapped and leaning against the packing-case wall. "*There you are*", she said. "*It's yours now!*". I couldn't believe my eyes! Joanie's lovely bicycle that Fred had kept in pristine condition for her, complete with its own pump, a basket on the front, and a carrying rack on the back – and it was a ladies free-wheel bike, not fixed wheel … was this really mine now? I hugged her so much, I was so thrilled. At last I could get rid of that boy's bike that had been the subject of so much ridicule! Joanie told me to unwrap it when I got back from Melbourne, then it would feel like a new one to me. I didn't mind one bit that it was not brand new, it was beautiful, and it had belonged to Joanie so it was really special.

We caught the train, and when we got to Melbourne we booked in to the Travellers' Aid again – the very last time that Joanie and Fred would be separated overnight, as they were actually paying passengers on the trip back so they had been allocated a cabin to occupy all together as a family. The next day we took the tram to the docks, and there was the SS Orontes, ready to board. We all went up the gangplank and helped Joanie and Fred settle into their cabin. Denise, as ever, was chuckling and happy, even though the sights and sounds must have been very strange to her. We explored the ship and then the announcement came that we were dreading, that all non-passengers must leave the ship. "*Goodbye, Titch*" whispered Fred as we hugged. "*Look after Mum, and be good*". The pain of saying goodbye was so acute we were all in tears. We wished them good luck, told them to write to us as often as possible, and then we had to tear ourselves away.

Standing on the dockside and watching the huge ship slowly pull away from the quay, the traditional coloured streamers breaking one by one, I wondered just how many more times in my life I would have to experience this sense of deep loss of people I loved. We watched as the ship disappeared out of sight and then sadly made our way back to the Travellers' Aid for one more night before we returned to Corowa. At least I had my hero, my wonderful brother Peter, for company and protection.

At the end of the academic year each class was awarded prizes for various examples of good work produced during the previous 12 months. At the end of 1953 I was thrilled when Miss Kerr announced that I had won the prize for the 'Neatest Geography Notebook'. I had never received any recognition for any work that I had done in class, so this meant a great deal to me. The prizes were presented at the final Morning Assembly of the term, and I was delighted to receive a wonderful glossy book of the Coronation of Queen Elizabeth II which had taken place in June of that year. The book was full of coloured photographs of the ceremony, the Crown Jewels, and all the Royal Family. I had been aware of a few jealous comments from other children since it had been announced that I had been awarded the prize, but I was totally unprepared for what happened that afternoon after the presentation.

We were all out on the sports field, when a boy from my class told me that Miss Kerr wanted to see me in the classroom. I went upstairs to the room where I had left my precious prize on my desk when I had gone down to the sports field. Miss Kerr was not there, but there were about five or six of my classmates in there, both boys and girls. I was suddenly grabbed from behind and forced to sit down at my desk. A boy then produced a small grass snake from behind him and dangled it, squirming furiously, in front of my face. "*We are going to make sure you never win a prize again*" he said threateningly. With that, whilst they held me in my chair, a boy took out a penknife and cut the head off the still-wriggling snake, and dripped the blood all over my new book. Once the snake stopped bleeding they threw it out of the window and ran out of the room, laughing loudly and threatening to cut **my** head off if I told anyone what they had done. I was so shocked that I sat there rigidly, my head swimming. I don't know how long I sat there. Then came the tears that wouldn't stop. I tried to clean the book up as best I could, but it was well and truly spoiled.

When I left the school, almost everyone had gone. I scurried to the cycle sheds, got on my bicycle and fled. It seemed like forever before I reached the sanctuary of the house and sat there trembling, cuddling Pash until Mum got home from work. I showed her the book and she was so disgusted at what had happened, she wanted to go straight to the school and make a complaint, but I begged her not to – I didn't want **my** head chopped off. When Peter came home from work he too was incensed, but I was so scared that I didn't want anyone to do anything. Fortunately it was the end of term, and I had no need to go back to school until the new term started after Christmas and the New Year. Mum resolved to replace the book for me but she was never able to find the same book, so I still have my bloodstained one.

Chapter 23 – Hard Work

The three of us – Peter, Mum and I – spent Christmas Day picnicking at the Boatshed. Mum and I cycled down, me on Joanie's lovely gift to me, her bicycle, and Peter took all the food down on his motorbike. He was the object of many admiring glances from the young ladies down there, looking especially handsome in his swimming trunks. He told Mum that he was really happy and that he didn't expect to be leaving Corowa for a while, especially now that he was engaged to Babs Rolton.

Shortly after the New Year, Peter came home from work, proudly driving a new car! He had decided, now that he was courting, that he should have something more suitable than a motorbike for taking Babs out, so he bought a Singer sports car. He was so proud of it, and I loved to ride in it around the town, and see the admiring glances that he and the car attracted. Unfortunately, one day when he took us out for a ride, the big end went on the car, so he treated himself to a brand new Austin A40 Somerset.

During the remainder of the school holidays, Peter asked Mum if she could get a few days off work as he wanted to take us on a camping holiday. I was really excited, as I had never camped before. Mum got the days off and we packed his car up with everything we would need. The Poidevins agreed to take care of Pash, our chooks, cats and birds, so we set off on a wonderful five days touring in Peter's new car around the surrounding area. We would wake up in the mornings to the sound of the kookaburras chortling their distinctive call all around us. We drove through Myrtleford and Bright to Omeo, then on to Bairnsdale, and Lakes Entrance. Peter slept in a small tent on his own and Mum and I shared a slightly larger one. Peter had borrowed the camping gear from a friend so we had everything we needed to make our adventure a comfortable one. On the day before we headed for home we saw a solitary kangaroo bounding across the fields in the distance … the only one that Mum and I saw during our whole time in Australia! The day after we left Omeo a bushfire swept through the town and all but wiped it out. We could see the smoke on the horizon but had no idea of how serious it was until we got back to Corowa and saw the newspapers.

Both Peter and I had acquired an Australian accent, not really by choice, but just by associating with people who spoke like that all the time, and Peter felt that he was being accepted more readily because of it. Mum, however, was stuck with her Lancashire accent, and when the farmers came in to the Council Office to pay their rates or on Council business some of them would immediately realise that she was not Australian and verbally abuse her, telling her to go back to England instead of taking a job that an Australian could do. Her response was to pick up various items from her desk, saying "*Well, this has 'Made in England' on it, and so does this, and so does this – if we are such bad people, how come you buy all our products?*". This, of course, did not endear her to these customers, but they usually left the office suitably chastened.

I returned to school with trepidation, not knowing whether I was going to be bullied again. However, because it was a new academic year some children were not moved up because of their slow progress, and I was delighted to find that some of my tormentors had to repeat the first year of High School. My dear friend Brenda was, however, steadfastly by my side. The incident with the book and the snake was never mentioned again.

One day at the end of February we received a letter from Joanie and Fred, letting us know that they had arrived back safely and were living once more with Fred's Mum. Mum replied immediately with all our news and we looked forward to their reply, knowing that it would take weeks.

Also in February that year the whole country was excited to be receiving a Royal Visit from Queen Elizabeth II and the Duke of Edinburgh. The school was decorated with Union Jacks and much of our class work was based on the Royal Visit. We had a map of Australia on the wall with the route of the Royal Party marked on it. Nationally, the Queen won the hearts of the Australian people. Peter asked Mum if she and I would like to go to Benalla to see the Queen, the nearest point to Corowa that she was due to visit. Mum leapt at the opportunity and we set out really early on 5th March, the day before my birthday. We joined the crowds of people lining the route and we were able to see the Royal Couple drive slowly past where we were standing. We waved our flags vigorously, delighted to have our Queen there before us. Mum took a photograph and managed to get a picture of the Duke's hand waving at the crowds, but also managing to cut off the rest of the smiling couple! Sadly, a lot of people in Corowa were annoyed at the cost of the Royal Visit and said that there must be better things to spend that money on. We ignored them – we had seen **our** Queen, and it was worth every penny!

Mum had seen an advertisement for a set of encyclopaedia in the newspaper, and she had ordered me a set as a present for my 13th birthday on 6th March. They were called Arthur Mee's Children's Encyclopaedia, and I have them still. They arrived one a month, which was the only way that she could afford to buy them for me. On one occasion I had prepared my History homework, an essay on Captain Cook, using these as a reference. The day after I submitted the homework I was told that I had to report to Mr Bryan's office after school. Again I found myself outside his office wondering what I had done wrong. When I got in there he called me a cheat and said that if I was caught copying another student's work again I would be expelled. What was he talking about? I had not cheated, I would never have dreamed of copying someone else's work. He threw my homework at me and asked me how come it was almost a carbon copy of another girl's work. He then showed me another piece of homework from one of my classmates, which I have to confess was very similar to mine … but why did they think that **I** was the cheat, why couldn't the other girl have somehow seen my work after I had finished it and copied **mine**? Mr Bryan told me to get out, so I fled from his office and cycled furiously home, crying all the way. I explained to Mum what had happened and the next day, without an appointment, she went to the school and insisted on seeing Mr Bryan. She asked him whether it had occurred to him that the other girl might be the cheat, or indeed, whether the other girl might have the same set of encyclopaedia to the one that I had. This had obviously not occurred to Mr Bryan, so he had the girl brought to his office and she was asked if she had Arthur Mee's Children's Encyclopaedia, to which she replied "*Yes, I use them all the time*". This solved the mystery, but Mr Bryan was angry at having been proved wrong – and the girl went back to class and told everyone that I had been in trouble because of cheating so it didn't really improve my status in the class!

One afternoon I decided to walk to the main road at the end of King Street to meet Peter as he came home from work. Mum was in the house getting tea for all of us. I walked down past the council yard to the corner, and there was no sign of Peter's car coming so I decided to walk a little way towards the town and get a lift back with him. Ahead of me I saw what looked like a heap of black clothes lying at the side of the road. As I neared it, I was horrified to see that it was my lovely Pash, mangled by a passing car. I ran home distraught and was sobbing so deeply that I couldn't get the words out to tell Mum what had happened. She cuddled me but I was inconsolable. By this time Peter was home and he had seen Pash and knew what the problem was. He got a sack and went back to where Pash lay, carefully put him in the sack and brought him home. We had a little burial service for him in the back garden and put a cross on the grave with his name on it. It took me a long time to get over the loss, and then one day Mum came home with a gorgeous black Cocker Spaniel puppy for me. I christened him Dusty, and from then on he was not allowed out without being on a lead.

A girl called Martina Kyprios from a Greek family, although in a year above me, was quite friendly towards me. Near the top end of Sanger Street her family had a milk bar, and Martina told me that they needed someone to help in the evenings. I went to enquire about the job, was interviewed on the spot, and I was delighted to be able to go home and tell Mum that I had got it. Mum made me go straight away to the nursery and tell them that I couldn't work there after school any more. Fortunately their son had reached an age where he was helping more and more with the business, so they asked me if I could still come at weekends, which I continued to do. The work in the shop was very hard, carting big demi-johns of syrup from the cold store into the shop, topping up all the dispensers for the various flavours of milk shakes, and scrubbing the floors to keep everywhere clean as it tended to get very sticky with spillages. Also, the hours at the milk bar were long, from 5pm to 11pm on Monday to Friday, but the pay was reasonable so I was pleased to have the job. I stayed at school between 4pm and 5pm to do my homework. Working these hours meant that I had to cycle home late at night, which I hated. Joanie had left me a pair of red Wellington boots when she had returned to England, and I loved them because they had fur around the top of them – I thought they were very smart. One night, I left the milk bar at 11pm and started to cycle home when the fur caught in the chain of my bike. I fell over sideways but couldn't free the fur, so I lay there trapped underneath the bike, struggling in the middle of the road. Three or four cars drove past me and completely ignored my plight and I was getting scared that eventually one would hit me. I don't know how long I struggled for but eventually a lady stopped – she helped me remove the boot and untangle the fur from the chain. When I got home Mum was really worried about where I had got to, but when I related the story to them, both she and Peter thought it was really funny. The sad thing was, the fur had to be cut off the boots which reduced them to pretty ordinary ones in my eyes!

We received another letter from Joanie and Fred telling us all about Denise's first birthday, and how Fred had been given his old job back at Evans, now Otis Lifts. This was a great relief, and we were pleased to receive all the other news about Fred's family. I asked Mum if I could reply to the letter and I wrote telling Joanie what had happened to the boots. I knew it would make her smile and I was able to laugh at it, too, although it had been very scary at the time.

Just prior to Anzac Day, 25th April, 1954 I was amazed to be told that I would be laying the High School's wreath at the Monument with Joy Miller, and that I had to be in smart uniform for the parade. I was so proud, and thought that I had at long last been accepted as an Australian. Joy and I rehearsed what we had to do and on the day it all went like clockwork. After the parade Mum wanted to take a photograph of us both with the wreath, so we posed at the Monument. I suddenly noticed a boy standing on the side of the road and my heart skipped a beat – it was

Tony Crisp, the boy from Whitehead Street that I had had a crush on when we lived opposite him. He came over to speak to me and asked if he could sit next to me at the pictures next time we went. Oh, bliss!! Mum stood nearby and asked him if she could take a photograph of him, which I still have. I think she wanted to record the moment when her youngest was asked for her first 'date'! I told Tony that I would be at the pictures the next night and so we sat and held hands during the films. I thought that I was in Seventh Heaven! However, it turned out to be a very temporary Heaven, as Tony must have decided that I was not going to be the love of his life and I never got the chance to hold hands with him again!

Not long after this I heard some really sad news – Tony had been involved in a shooting accident. He and a friend were out shooting rabbits, and his friend had the safety catch off on his shotgun – as they were climbing through a wire fence the friend's shotgun had gone off, injuring Tony in the back. From then on he was paralysed from the waist down and was confined to a wheelchair. I was able to catch up with him by telephone many years later and I was flattered that he remembered me.

Now that I was 13, Mum decided that I should have my hair permed. I remember going to the hairdressers and having curlers put into my hair that were attached to electrical connections on a bar that stretched across the ceiling. It looked like something out of a science fiction film, and I emerged from the hairdressers with hair that looked like an explosion in a mattress factory! I was, however, very pleased with it as I had had straight hair all my life and to have curls was, I believed, very 'grown up'. We were due to go to one of the Corowa Barn Dances and for the first time I would not be wearing trousers. Mum had bought me a pretty yellow dress that crossed over at the bust and tied at the back. Unfortunately, I had no bust at that time so Mum decided that nature needed some help. She bought me my first bra and when we were getting ready for the Barn Dance, she tucked a rolled-up stocking into each cup – as I surveyed the result in the mirror I was quite pleased with the reflection.

Peter took us to the Literary Institute in his car and I was so looking forward to the Barn Dance. When I got into the hall, however, it occurred to me that if I joined in the dances I might just lose the rolled-up stockings that gave me the perfect shape! This destroyed my confidence completely so I sat disconsolately on the straw bales, watching everyone having fun. Peter came over and insisted I dance with him, so he whirled me onto the floor, whilst all the time I kept an eye on my newly-acquired bust. What happened next was totally unexpected – far from falling out, the rolled-up stockings stayed firmly in place ... but my waist-petticoat slipped gracefully down my legs, tripping me up as I danced! I was mortified. I stepped out of it, screwed it up into a ball, and ran back to the straw bales whilst most of the people on the floor laughed at my discomfiture. I sat there crying, and when Peter came over I begged him to take me home, which he did. I never lived that episode down, and Peter often used to tease me by saying things like "*I hear you 'slipped' up at the Barn Dance the other night, Titch!*". My embarrassment did not end there, however, as Mum insisted that I wear the bra now that I had one, and she took great delight in telling her work colleagues and the people that we babysat for "*She's all grown up now, she is wearing her first bra*" – not the best way to instil confidence into an awkward teenager!

The Council were building about a dozen council houses in Corowa, and they advertised this fact by inviting people who wanted to be allocated one to put their names forward to Mr Tasker. Mum was amongst the first to apply, and when the houses were finished there was great excitement at the coming allocation. So many people had applied that there was to be a lottery held one evening at the Council Offices. We had been to see the finished houses and compared to what we had, they were lovely. They were also closer in to Corowa than where we were living, which would have been so much more convenient for Mum's work, and both my school and workplaces. The room was crowded, very hot and with many people smoking. There was an air of excitement that you could almost touch. The names all went into a tombola barrel, and they were withdrawn one by one. We were heartbroken when our name didn't get picked out. Everyone who had been allocated a house was celebrating, hugging their friends and relatives, but we couldn't have been more demoralised.

The next day Mum went into work, and the talk was all about the lottery. Mum expressed her disappointment at not being picked and was astounded to be told by Mr Tasker that her name had not gone into the tombola barrel anyway! When she asked why not, he said "*Well, you already have a council house, why would you want another?*". Mum was shaken to the core – had Mr Tasker told her this before the lottery she would at least have had the chance to point out to him that the council house that we lived in had been due for demolition before we moved in and was not really a fit place to live. She put this point to him and he replied "*Well, you were grateful enough for it when you had nowhere else to go*". Mum asked him if anyone else's name had been withdrawn before the lottery and he confirmed that hers was the only one.

Having spent three and a half years being browbeaten and abused in this small town, Mum had come to the end of her tether. This discrimination, more than anything else, fired her determination to return to England. She was not prepared to take any more. That night she told me that we were going to save every penny in order to get back home. She knew that she would have to pay two adult fares back as I was now over 12 years old, the cut-off age for a child fare. I was upset to see Mum so angry, but I resolved that I would also save as much as possible to help towards the fares.

Chapter 24 – On our own again

Peter's engagement to Babs Rolton came to an end and he became restless. He was a fully-qualified electrician, so he decided to go off on his own to find work. On the day that Peter left we said our tearful farewells and he promised that he would keep in touch. He planned to stay in New South Wales, probably in Sydney, and said he would come back to see us whenever he could. The house seemed empty without him; this meant that I had to become 'the man of the house' again, and tackle the jobs like chopping the firewood, emptying the cesspit, painting the chook pen with sump oil and gardening. I was still working at the café every weekday evening and at the nursery at the weekends. I was also babysitting regularly for the Rippingales on weekend evenings. Mum was working at the Council Offices, and also babysitting as much as possible. We didn't go to the pictures any more, and treats like holidays and coach trips were sacrificed in order to save all our spare money for the fare back to England.

As a child, no-one had made me clean my teeth regularly and the result of this was that my teeth deteriorated, especially with no regular check-ups in Australia as we couldn't afford them. Around this time I suffered a really bad toothache and had eventually to go to the dentist in Sanger Street. He took a look at my teeth, identified the troublesome one and said it had to come out. I told him that I didn't have enough money for the extraction so he asked me how much I did have. When I told him he said that he could remove the tooth without anaesthetic for that, so I agreed. I have never experienced such pain since I injured my leg when I was seven, and it left me terrified of dentists. This fear finally left me after I returned to England and had once again to go for emergency treatment, but this time the dentist couldn't have been more kind ... and I didn't have to pay!

By August Mum had saved enough money for our fares so she went to the travel agent and booked our passage on a boat called the SS 'Esperance Bay' (11,800 tons), a small liner of the Shaw Savill and Albion Line. She had been built in 1922, and would be making her final voyage back to England where she was to be broken up. She was due to sail on Monday, 22nd November that year, 1954. We were thrilled to bits, and Mum immediately wrote to Joanie and Fred to let them know that we would be back home with them in the not-too-distant future.

As we neared November, Mum was busily selling some of our furniture that we could manage without and packing up our personal effects that we wanted to take back with us in our faithful old sea-chest and some tea chests. They were due to be collected early in November and stored in a warehouse in Melbourne until they could be loaded onto the 'Esperance Bay'. She decided that we would keep our bicycles until the last minute as we had no other means of transport from and to King Street. I could feel the excitement building inside me. I couldn't believe that I would soon be on British soil again. My savings were building up and I was proud that at least Mum and I would have a reasonable amount of spend money on the return trip, as she had exhausted all her savings on the fares. Mum told Mr Bryan, the Headmaster, that I would be leaving the school on Friday 19th November, and asked him if he could provide a letter that she could take to the Education Authorities in England when we got back in order to get me placed into the right school. (As I had left England before I had taken the 11-plus examination which would have placed me either in a Grammar School or a Secondary Modern School, it was essential for the English authorities to have some guidelines on my academic ability in order to make their decision.)

Mum told Mr Tasker at the Council Offices that she would be leaving on 19th November so that he had time to find a replacement for her. She gave notice that we would vacate the house in King Street on Sunday, 21st November. We also told all the families that we babysat for that we would soon be leaving. Brenda was sad that I was going, but we made plans to keep in touch with each other by letter. She let me ride her horse, Trixie, a lot, as I'm sure she realised that I wouldn't get much opportunity to ride in London.

Apart from Brenda, my classmates were not terribly interested in the fact that I was leaving. There was no-one else there that I particularly wanted to keep in touch with so the parting with them was not a sad prospect. It was different with Brenda, though. She had been my rock, my support at school, and I knew that I would miss her dreadfully. I didn't know if I would ever see her again.

Peter came home for a weekend in October, and although he knew that we were saving hard, he was surprised that we would be leaving so soon as he didn't realise that we would achieve so quickly the target sum needed to book our passages home. He was doing well in his electrician's employment, and he had to return to his work. He had had his photograph taken at a Studio in Corowa, and he gave Mum and I a postcard sized photograph each, on the back of which he had written a message. He also gave Mum a much larger one to have framed when we got back to England. I loved the photo, he looked so handsome on it, and I still have it. He promised that he would come back the weekend before we were due to leave to say good-bye.

Mum had sold our bicycles to a man who agreed that we could keep them until the day before we left. She had also found homes for all our pets. Dusty, my dog, was going next door to live with the Poidevins. They were also going to have the chooks, and Mrs Maclean was going to have the birds and the cats, so that took care of the whole menagerie.

On Friday, 19th November, the day that I left school, I went round to say goodbye to all the teachers, who wished me well. I had been told to report to Mr Bryan's office after school, so again I found myself waiting to be called in. This time, though, there was no trepidation as I knew I had done nothing wrong. When he called me in he gave me an envelope for Mum and then surprised me by giving me a peck on the cheek, shaking my hand, and wishing me good luck. It was the only time I saw him as a human being and not as an ogre!

I made my way to Mum's office to give her the envelope, and say goodbye to her work colleagues, but unbeknown to me Mum had had a bombshell dropped in her lap that day. A telegram had arrived for her from the Shaw Savill office in Melbourne, and as the Post Office knew that she worked at the Council Offices they had delivered it there instead of the house, which turned out to be a blessing for us, it being a Friday afternoon. The telegram said that as there was a dock strike in Melbourne the 'Esperance Bay' was unable to sail, and that we should not go to Melbourne until we heard further. Poor Mum, after nearly four years of a difficult existence in an unwelcoming country, right at the last minute things were still going wrong for her. She had apparently sat down and cried when she read the telegram … what was she to do? The house was practically empty, she had given notice to leave it, and she was due to leave her job that day. I had left school, and the only money we had was my savings, so staying in an hotel for an indefinite period was out of the question. Her work colleagues rallied round, and provided her with a solution. Mr Tasker said that Mum could continue to work for as long as she needed to, because she could train her replacement in that time, but plans were in place to demolish the King Street house because they needed to add the space to the council yard next door, so we **had** to vacate it. Winsley came back from her lunch break and told Mum that she had spoken to her parents, and they had invited us to stay with them for as long as it took. When I arrived at the Council Offices and heard what was happening, I too was in tears. We had both been so looking forward to leaving, to getting back to England and seeing Joanie, Fred and Denise again, and to be amongst friends – this was a bitter blow.

Winsley asked me to go to her home in Honour Avenue to see her Mum, Aunty Cora, and she would tell me what the arrangements were. I cycled to the house, knocked on the door … an entered into the most loving, happy home that I have ever stayed in! Aunty Cora gave me a big cuddle and told me not to worry, everything would be alright. She had had another son Andrew just before Denise had been born the previous year so there were nine people already living in this home, but it didn't feel overcrowded because everyone was loved equally by this amazing, generous, lovely lady who was prepared to share all she had with us. Mum cycled to the house with Winsley after work, and she, too, was welcomed with open arms by Aunty Cora and Uncle Duff. We were shown where we could sleep (it had been necessary to re-arrange the family's sleeping arrangements because of us!), and by the time Mum and I left the house we were both feeling a lot happier after this unexpected shock.

We cycled back to King Street and did the final packing and clearing up. Fortunately we only had a case each as all our other personal effects had gone into storage some weeks before. Mum put the letter from Mr Bryan in her case without opening it. Peter arrived on the Saturday and was amazed at what had happened to us in the past couple of days! He was so relieved that we had found solutions to the problems, though he was not at all surprised that Aunty Cora and Uncle Duff had so generously stepped in to help, as he had come to know the family well when he was seeing Winsley and knew how lovely they were. He told us that he had planned to take us to Melbourne on the Sunday as a surprise, so that we wouldn't have needed to catch the train, which would have been lovely. He promised that he would return as often as he could before we left as none of us knew when that would be, so we said our goodbyes on the Sunday, not knowing if we would see him again before we left for Melbourne. Before he left he gave us each a present – to me he gave a beautiful manicure set in a red leather case (which, although battered by years of use, is still one of my most treasured possessions), and for Mum he had bought a lovely black leather handbag. I had that familiar knot in my stomach as I clung to him, not wanting to part from him yet again. He promised that one day he would come back to see me in England, which cheered me up a lot.

Although Mum continued to work, she felt that it was not necessary for me to return to school as she hoped it would only be a few days before the dock strike was over. I decided that I would try to earn some more money, so on the day that we should have sailed I went to the Kyprios' café to see if I could continue there. They had already found a replacement for me so I was told no. I also tried the nursery, but they were fully staffed too. Then I boldly went into the Nicholson & Lethbridge office and asked to see Mr Lethbridge. He was surprised to see me as he thought we had left Corowa the previous day, but when I explained what had happened and told him that we were still available for babysitting until we were given a new sailing date, he seemed quite pleased. He said he would get in touch with Mum at the Council Offices when he needed a babysitter. This gave me a bit more confidence, so I walked up to Maples and saw Mr Rippingale. He too was surprised to see me, but also said he would get in touch if he needed us. They were both true to their word and so we were able to earn some extra money, which Mum was determined to pay to Aunty Cora and Uncle Duff for our keep.

The days turned into weeks. In the end, we spent a month enveloped in the warmth and love of this truly magnificent family. They made what would have been a terrible time for us into a happy, laughing, cheerful and enjoyable experience and we will never be able to repay them for all their kindness and generosity, made all the more incredible because they refused to accept a penny from us, saying that we needed all the money we had to finance the move back to England.

Peter came to visit three weeks after we had moved in with the Howard family. He was apologetic that he had not been able to come before, and surprised that we were still there. He was only able to stay for a few hours, and then came the inevitable sadness at parting again. This time I really did have a feeling that it would be the last time we would see him, at least for some considerable time. I clung tightly to him, and so did Mum.

Another telegram arrived for Mum on 16th December, this time with good news. The ship was due to sail on Tuesday, 21st December, 1954 at 4pm. At last! We only had a few days to go, then we could head for Melbourne.

Mum wrote immediately to Peter and to Joanie to tell them the news. She told Mr Tasker that she could only work one more day, and he accepted that. I walked down to see Mr Lethbridge and Mr Rippingale to say my goodbyes.

Mum decided that we would travel to Melbourne on the morning of the day we sailed to save the cost of a night's stay at the Travellers' Aid. The train left early in the morning, and Brenda promised to come to the railway station to say goodbye if I woke her up. Saying goodbye to Aunty Cora, Uncle Duff and the family was so tough. I had come to love them all as much as I loved my own family, but as much as it hurt the time had come to say farewell to this wonderful, warm and loving lady and her equally wonderful husband and family. I shall always remain truly grateful for their gesture of friendship at a time when we found ourselves in that awful predicament.

Mum left each of the children some money as a Christmas present, the only way she could think of to show our deep and lasting gratitude.

Brenda lived just around the corner from where Aunty Cora lived, and quite near to the train station. We walked to her house and Mum waited outside with the cases. I crept into the sleepout at the back where Brenda was sleeping. I woke her up gently ... it was still only 5am. She sat up in bed and gave me a hug. She also gave me a book as a parting present called 'Castle Secrets' by Jean Seivright. I still have it and have lost count of the number of times that I have read it. She was very sleepy and didn't want to get out of bed, so I told her not to worry about coming to the train station. We hugged each other again and then I left. I am still amazed at the loyalty and friendship she gave me during those four years, considering all the opposition I had faced from the other children at school, and I am still blessed with her friendship over 50 years later.

Mum and I boarded the train, and were relieved as the town that had caused us so much hurt and pain receded into the distance. Apart from leaving Brenda and Aunty Cora and her family behind, we had no regrets at heading as far away from Corowa as we could get.

Part 4

The Journey Home

Chapter 25 – We are on our way back!

We arrived in Melbourne quite early and made our way to the docks. The 'Esperance Bay' was tied up at the quay and there was a lot of activity, loading luggage onto the ship. We fervently hoped that our sea chest and our tea chests were amongst the ones being loaded. I was bursting with excitement and so wanted to get on board and start our journey, but we were not allowed on the ship until after lunch. It was the strangest sensation, sitting on our cases on the quayside just as we had done nearly four years ago when we were waiting to be collected by the farmer. We were lost in silent thought about the last four years, what we had gone through and how we had survived it. Mum was 55 years old, and all the tougher for the experience. I was nearly 14 years old – what I had learned in that time had made an adult out of me early, and equipped me better than most children to deal with whatever life was to throw at me in the future.

We were finally allowed on board and given our cabin number. The memories of the journey out to Australia came flooding back as we made our way through the thrumming sound of the engines and the smell of diesel into the bowels of the ship to find our cabin. When we found it, it turned out to be another six-berth one, so we prepared ourselves for another cramped and crowded trip. However, we were pleasantly surprised to be joined by a young girl called Joan who told us that she had heard from the Purser that there were only going to be the three of us in the cabin, so we could spread out a bit. We unpacked and settled in, then went to explore the rest of the vessel that would be our home for the next six weeks. As the 'Esperance Bay' was a small ship she would take longer to reach England than the larger, faster passenger liners.

We quickly discovered that there were no First Class areas. The whole ship was at our disposal. There was only one dining room and we found where we were to sit, having been allocated the first sitting for all meals. My chair was covered in a white loose cover and I wondered why. I later discovered that the ship's Surgeon used my seat at the second sitting, and he needed protection for his white uniform. We also noticed that there was no swimming pool, which was quite a blow. Where would they perform the 'Crossing the Line Ceremony'? No matter, we were heading home and that was the important thing.

Shortly before 4pm there came the announcement that all non-passengers must leave the ship. Then came the deafening ship's horn signalling the start of the voyage – followed by the breaking of all the streamers that had been thrown from the ship to the quayside as the ship moved away from the dock. I had always found this so heartbreaking on previous occasions, but this time it felt like a release from a prison's chains. We stood on the deck for ages watching Melbourne fade into the distance, breathing huge sighs of relief – it was all over, and a familiar life awaited us back at home.

We went into the lounge for a cup of tea and sat with a family, the Robinsons. Once we had got chatting to them we became aware that they had had a similar experience to us. I instantly made friends with their daughter Penelope, a girl slightly older than me. The Robinsons had been talking to another family, who had also been discriminated against where they had been living in Australia ... and it became like a huge snowball, as one by one everyone shared their experiences of the unfair treatment and verbal abuse that they had received. We had been told by the locals in Corowa to 'go to a big city and lose ourselves there where we would not be so obvious', but on this ship there were families and single people from all over Australia, all fleeing from the same sort of harsh treatment. It turned out that all the passengers except for four Australians who were going to England on a working holiday, were disillusioned immigrants who couldn't wait to get back to the Mother Country. To my eternal shame, those four Australians were ostracised by all the other passengers, and their voyage must have been awful, so strong was the feeling of contempt that they were shown.

Our first stop was at Adelaide, but we didn't disembark – we had seen enough of Australia and we just wanted to get on with the journey. More passengers embarked, all with similar tales of their experiences.

A circular canvas swimming pool about 15 feet across had been erected so thankfully we had somewhere to swim, as the weather was very hot. We were served ice cream and salt tablets to counteract the effects of the heat. Then we had to cross the Great Australian Bight, and this is where my old friend sea-sickness revisited me – I was so sick that I had to retreat to the cabin and stay there for 24 hours! Joan joined me there and we suffered together. However, after a day in bed I bounced back, and had no more sea-sickness problems. Joan took a little longer, but she too was soon back on her feet. Mum, bless her, ever the good sailor, had absolutely no ill-effects at all.

We arrived at Perth, and again we chose not to disembark. More disillusioned immigrants boarded, and we all blended together in one mass of moans and groans about Australia – I think we were what Australians would call the original 'whingeing poms'! The four Australians on board had by this time learned that they were not going to be very popular, and kept out of the way.

Mum had seen a notice on board advertising a camel train trip along the Suez Canal, disembarking at Suez and rejoining the ship at Port Said. It was quite expensive but she felt it would be educational as we would see pyramids and temples en route, so we decided to save our money for that. We left Perth late on Christmas Eve, with everyone in a very happy mood. We knew that we would celebrate Christmas and the New Year during the ten days we had at sea without a stop, and during this time there would also be the 'Crossing the Line Ceremony', so it would be full of excitement even though there was no land in sight.

The Christmas Eve meal was followed by entertainment, and we all went to bed happily anticipating Christmas Day ... and what a day it was! There were games, fancy dress competitions, whist drives and bridge, deck quoits, deck tennis – all the old skills came back! Mum and I went to Church in the morning, there was a buffet lunch, and a superb traditional Christmas Dinner in the evening followed by more entertainment.

It was rapidly becoming clear that this was a very sentimental journey for all the crew, being the last that the 'Esperance Bay' would ever make, so they seemed to be putting great effort into making it memorable for us all. Tommy, our Table Steward, and I developed a good relationship, and I would often tease him by hanging around deliberately with my meal for too long so that he started panicking about getting the table ready for the Surgeon at the next sitting. The crew were allowed to fraternise with the passengers, and Tommy and I would often swim together, where he would get his own back by regularly ducking me. He was Irish, a lot older than me so it was never even close to a romance (I was still only 13!), but it was a great friendship. Our Cabin Steward was Maltese, and very good looking. Once when I returned to the cabin for something, he and Joan were in a very passionate clinch – I retreated embarrassed and always knocked on the door whenever I went to the cabin after that!

The 'Crossing the Line Ceremony' was great fun, with everyone knowing what to expect and willingly joining in. This time the Captain was King Neptune, and he was a real sport. After I had received my peck on the cheek from him I got thrown in the water and was rapidly joined by Mum. It was a day full of fun that I shall never forget.

The Robinson family were very keen on whist, which I had never played so they offered to teach me and we spent a lot of time in the lounge playing cards. Penelope and I entered into the deck quoits and deck tennis competitions. The daily tote of the miles travelled the previous day was won by Mum on one occasion, and every day was an enjoyable experience.

New Year's Eve was a magnificent night, with a huge Fancy Dress Ball. Mum dressed me up as a fortune teller, even managing to get some cocoa from the galley to darken my skin. I didn't win a prize, but I **was** impressed by the young couple that won First Prize. They went as 'Adam and Eve', and their costume was so simple it was bound to be a winner. No, they weren't naked, but she had a very skimpy flesh-coloured bikini on, and he wore a very skimpy pair of flesh-coloured swimming trunks, onto which they had stitched, in all the appropriate places, fig leaves made from crepe paper – it truly looked realistic! Mum and I had no doubt that this brand new year, 1955, was going to prove to be better than any of the last four years had been.

Chapter 26 – Trouble Brewing

At the end of our ten days at sea, we docked at Colombo in Ceylon. As we had done quite a comprehensive tour of the island on the voyage out to Australia, we decided just to explore the city of Colombo with Joan. We spent a pleasant few hours wandering around, we had tea in a restaurant and then returned to the boat. We sailed that evening and headed for Aden, then Suez. I was so excited, looking forward to the camel trip along the Suez Canal. A meeting was held that evening for all the people who had booked the camel ride – about 40 people had booked to go on it. The Officers who were due to go with us explained what we would be seeing, that we would be camping in tents overnight and have our food cooked by Arabs using their own recipes – it was going to be wonderful!

The next morning a notice went up to say that the trip from Suez to Port Said by camel had been cancelled, and that a meeting would be held in the lounge that afternoon to explain why, and to refund any monies paid. We were all so disappointed, as the meeting the previous evening had whetted our appetites for all the strange sights we were due to see.

We assembled in the lounge and the Senior Officer conducting the meeting explained that the area was a strategically important one, and that there were increasing hostilities taking place. There had been an assassination attempt on President Nasser's life in October 1954, and ever since the region had been quite volatile. News had just been received that things were likely to get worse and it was advised that the trip be cancelled. This was, of course, the very beginning of the Suez Crisis, which finally came to a head in July, 1956 when Nasser nationalised the Canal. We didn't realise this, though, and there was a lot of dissatisfaction at the meeting. The Officer was firm, there was no possibility of putting people's lives at risk, the money was refunded – and that was the end of it. Looking back I feel that this was absolutely the right decision but it was so disappointing at the time.

We moored at Suez, but we didn't disembark – I think we had all been made nervous by what we had been told. It was fun watching the 'bum-boats' selling their wares, and we left Suez, making our way sedately up the Suez Canal to Port Said.

When we reached Port Said Joan said she would like to see the market, so we all went together. This entailed another ride in a rickshaw each, and we giggled as the strong young lads manoeuvred their way between the traffic, which was truly chaotic! We had a bit more courage this time, knowing what to expect, so we wandered round the hundreds of stalls. Joan asked me to go and look at a spice stall with her so we wandered off. I hadn't noticed that Mum had disappeared for a few minutes but when she rejoined us she was carrying a bag. I asked her what she had bought and she said she would show me when we got back to the ship, so I put it out of my mind. Another rickshaw ride returned us to the quay and we went up the gangway back on board.

When we got to the cabin Mum put her arms around me, gave me a cuddle, and said that she knew that I had been disappointed about not doing the camel trip, so she had bought me a present to make up for it. Then she handed me the bag that she had acquired at the market. I opened it and was delighted to see inside a set of the beautiful black silk pyjamas that I had so admired, but couldn't afford, on the journey out. They were richly embroidered with dragons, and the set consisted of matching pyjamas, dressing gown and slippers, the slippers edged with white fur. I was so thrilled with them ... and it was years before I actually realised that it was **my** savings that had paid for them! Never mind, they were beautiful, and I had wanted a set since I had first seen them four years ago.

After leaving Port Said we made our way through the beautifully calm Mediterranean Sea, heading for our next port of call, Malta. We had booked a tour of the island, but Joan had told us that she didn't want to go ashore this time so we went on our own. The ship moored in the harbour at Valletta, and Mum and I had to go ashore in one of the lovely Maltese traditional boats called Dghajsas with brightly painted prows, rowed by a Maltese man in national dress. We got to the bottom of the Barrakka Lift which took us up to the old fort and the Upper Barrakka Gardens from where the view over the Grand Harbour was spectacular. We boarded a coach for the tour and visited Sliema, Mdina (the historical capital of Malta) and other towns along the route. We were struck by how 'British' everything was. The policemen were in the same uniform as in the UK, the telephone boxes were the familiar bright red ones that you saw all over the British Isles, and the shops had familiar names, too. It is a pretty island, and we thoroughly enjoyed the reminders that 'home' was on the horizon! Our last scheduled visit was to the Catacombs at Rabat. These were very scary as they had been used for all sorts of purposes, including a secret place of worship for early Christians until Constantine I recognised Christianity and the persecution of Christians ceased. The Romans also used them to bury their dead, and there were skulls and skeletons in niches everywhere. St Paul supposedly spent three months in the Catacombs when he landed on Malta in 60AD. I was glad to come back up into the sunlight!

The coach dropped us off at St John's Cathedral in Valletta, so we decided to have a look round. The Cathedral was magnificent and it took us some considerable time to gaze in wonder at its many treasures, and wall and ceiling paintings. When we emerged we realised that we still had a couple of hours before we needed to be back on the ship so we took one of the traditional horse-drawn carriages, called Karrozzins, on a tour round the city. It was such fun, we laughed all the time, and our guide was brilliant, pointing out places of interest. It was not expensive, and worth every penny to get a good look at this, our last port of call before arriving back in England. The carriage dropped us off at the Upper Barrakka Gardens, where we went down to sea level in the lift and caught a Dghajsa back to the ship.

When we got back on board, we went to the cabin to freshen up. Joan wasn't there, so we went for a walk around the decks to see if we could see her sunbathing. There was no sign of her anywhere. We were beginning to panic a little – where could she be? About 10 minutes before we were due to sail, we went to the Purser's Office to report that we couldn't find her. He looked at his lists which revealed that she had disembarked early in the afternoon. He said that if she missed the ship, that would be her problem. We were very worried, but the ship set sail without her. We learned later that she had jumped ship to be with our Cabin Steward, whose employment had finished when we arrived at Malta. He could not have known that she was planning to do this, as we also learned afterwards that he was married with a family! He apparently had viewed their affair as just a shipboard romance and had no intention of spending his future with her. Unfortunately – or fortunately, I'm not sure – the Maltese Government would not let her stay, and she was flown back to Birmingham, arriving in the UK several days before we did! (A few weeks later we received a letter from her explaining what had happened, and although Mum replied, that was the last contact that we had with her.)

Once it had been established that Joan was not coming back on board, the Purser asked us to pack up all her things up (which she had left so as not to alert us to the fact that she planned to jump ship), and the Purser took possession of her case. The sudden departure of our cabin mate meant that we had the whole cabin to ourselves for the remainder of the journey, which was great.

There was an air of great excitement on board. Everyone was impatient for our journey to finish. It was getting very sentimental, as all the crew and passengers knew that this was the very last voyage of the dear old 'Esperance Bay'. An old tub she may have been, but she had done us proud. It had been a happy band of people joining together to enjoy their journey back to the land they loved. The four Australians on board had kept themselves very discreetly in the background, and the resentment and hatred shown to them at first diminished noticeably over the length of the voyage.

We sailed past Gibraltar in the early hours one morning, and many people went up on deck to see the beautiful sight of the Rock lit up. It was another piece of 'Great Britain' that we all yearned for, and it cheered us up tremendously. We then sailed, on calm seas, round the south-western end of Portugal and up the Portuguese coast.

Once again we had to face the churning seas of the Bay of Biscay but I was not sea-sick this time, although a lot of people were. The crockery was sliding across the tables, held on only by the lips at the edges of the tables designed to keep everything from falling. We were into much colder climes, and it was a challenge to get the beef tea into you in the mornings before most of it slopped out of the cup!

The journey was almost over. The Brest Peninsula slipped past us, and we prepared for our Landfall Dinner. What a truly sentimental, wonderful evening that was. The crew dined with us, we sang songs, and the meal was superb. Everyone was tearful, and in the lounge afterwards the Captain thanked us all for being the 'perfect passengers' to end the ship's long record of sterling service as not only a passenger liner, but as an armed merchant cruiser between 1939 and 1941. We exchanged addresses with the dear friends that we had made on the trip, and went to bed ready to wake up to the day that we had all been waiting for.

The next day everyone was up on deck early to get the first sight of 'The Needles' on the Isle of Wight. A huge cheer went up as they came into view! Then we rounded the Isle of Wight, sailed up The Solent, and watched as the liner eased herself, with the help of the tugboats, into her berth at Southampton Docks. Mum and I scanned the waiting crowd for a glimpse of Joanie and Fred and then we caught sight of them, with Denise waving frantically at us. I looked at Mum and once more saw the silent tears from this amazing lady who had ensured our survival in the most difficult time of our lives ... and realised that my cheeks, too, were wet.

The gangway went down, and eventually Joanie, Fred and Denise managed to get on board along with the many other friends and family who had come to meet loved ones. We flung ourselves into each other's arms, and I heard the familiar voice of Fred saying "*Welcome home, Titch*!". Denise was now 20 months old and just as beautiful as ever. I hugged Joanie so tightly, I think I nearly suffocated her! It was then that I appreciated just how much I had missed them all.

We went down to the cabin to get our belongings, and on the way back up to the deck we said our farewells to the many friends that we had made on board.

Finally, we made our way down the gangway and set our feet on the soil of England ... home at last!

Part Five

Postscript

Mum

Joanie had found Mum and me a bedsit in Camberwell, and as soon as we had settled in, Mum went to the Law Courts to see if they would give her a job. Her previous employment there was well-documented so she was offered a post straight away. She worked there until she was 60, and then went to work for Crescent-Webb, an engineering company in Borough High Street, Southwark. She stayed until she was 65, and then eventually moved out to Bury St Edmunds to be near me. That didn't last very long, though – my Father died in 1967 and Mum contacted his lifelong friend, Charlie Clout, from the Navy (who had been best man at their wedding) to give him the sad news. Uncle Charlie had lost his wife a few years previously so he wrote back to Mum, and a romance started that was to last ten years until Uncle Charlie died. Mum moved down to Portsmouth to live near him, but after his death she moved back up to Leiston in Suffolk to be near me again.

Mum lived to be 100 years old. This amazing, indomitable old lady managed to live on her own until she was 98, when she decided that she wanted more company, so she moved into an old people's home in Norwich where I was able to see her every day until she died in November, 1999. Had she lived for two more months, she would have been almost unique as someone who had lived in three centuries – the 1800's, the 1900's and the 2000's, but I think that she had decided that reaching 100 was enough. Her spirit and courage never left her, and I will always be grateful for the strength and determination that she passed on to me – it has stood me in good stead all my adult life.

Peter

During the early part of 1955, Peter continued working in New South Wales and he was so successful that he saved up enough money to return to England in April of that year. Mum and I went to Southampton to meet him off the SS 'Castel Felice' (12,800 tons), a small liner belonging to the Sitmar Line, and I just clung to him, so pleased was I to see him again. It felt so right for us all to be back together. I still adored him, he was so handsome, and all my girl friends at school wanted to meet him after seeing his photograph that I still carried everywhere with me. He got a job in the menswear department at Jones and Higgins, a big department store in Peckham Rye, and they asked him if he would model some of their clothes for their catalogue. He did the work for the money but he didn't enjoy it, so there was no way he wanted to pursue male modelling as a career!

Peter made friends with an Australian, Kevin, and between them they bought a 38ft yacht which was moored in St Catherine's Dock in London, the plan being to sail it back to Australia together. The yacht was a very old, famous one called the 'Foam', and for many years it had been used to take the contraband from the famous old clipper ship the 'Cutty Sark' to the shore. I spent many hours scrubbing the decks with wire wool, and Peter and Kevin worked hard until she was in pristine condition and nearly ready to sail ... and then the unexpected happened. Kevin met Heather, an Australian girl in London – he fell in love, married her, and decided to stay in England. This left Peter with no-one to sail the boat back with him so he reluctantly sold the 'Foam'. I was so upset as he had promised me a trip on the yacht before they left as a reward for all my hard work, but it was never to happen.

Peter knew that if he stayed in England for any longer than two years, he would have to do British National Service for two years. As he had done National Service in Australia for three months and hated every minute of it, there was no way that he was going to stay and do some more in England, so after 22 months he left for Australia from Southampton on the SS Orcades (28,500 tons). Once again I found myself saying goodbye to someone I loved. I was 16 years old, and this time I really didn't know when I would see him again – I certainly thought that I would not be going back to Australia ... ever! If I had known just how long it would be before I saw him again, I think I would have moved heaven and earth to keep him in England.

On the trip back, Peter met and subsequently married his first wife. He built his own concrete-hulled yacht in Australia, and he and his wife sailed the Great Barrier Reef with clients on fishing trips. They had a daughter, and his wife decided it was better for her to be onshore.

We had letters from his wife's Mother for a while, but then the marriage broke up and the news stopped coming. Despite all our efforts we could not find where Peter was. Mum was distraught, and as the years drifted by, she began to wonder if he was still alive.

25 years later my daughter Wendy, then aged 16, went to Australia to spend six months with Brenda. Before she left, Mum said to her *"If you get the chance to look for your Uncle Peter, please try to find him for me"*. When I heard this, I was concerned – I had visions of some awful Australian being approached by my daughter, and him seizing on the opportunity to get close to this beautiful 16 year old! I told Wendy of my fears, and said to her *"If you think you have found Uncle Peter, before you do anything else, ask him what he used to call his younger sister (me) when she was a child. If you get the answer "Titch", you will know that you have found him"*. Wendy must have inherited some of Mum's determination, because she started alphabetically with the Adelaide telephone directory, and telephoned all the P. Bakers, P. J. Bakers, the Peter Bakers, and all the Peter John Bakers that she could find in the telephone books. Some thought it was a practical joke, some thought she was from a TV programme, some were very helpful and gave her numbers of other P. Bakers that they knew, but she met with no success ... that is, until she got to the Brisbane telephone directory.

On my birthday, March 6th, 1981, Wendy rang a P. J. Baker in Brisbane. The conversation went something like this: *"Hello, I'm trying to locate my Uncle Peter Baker who has been in Australia for over 20 years, and I was wondering if it might be you? He would be in his late forties, and he has an older sister called Joan and a younger sister called*

Dorothy" to which Peter replied "*Well, I might just be the person you are looking for*!". Wendy then said "*Before we go any further, please can you tell me what you used to call your younger sister?*" and Peter replied "*Oh, you mean 'Titch'!*". The outcome of this was that Wendy was invited to Brisbane, a trip she subsequently made, and we were back in touch with my beloved Peter! Apparently, after Peter put the phone down, he said to Val, a New Zealander who was soon to be his second wife "*I need a scotch – I think my family have found me!*". Wendy rang me straight away to give me the good news, and I rang Mum, who was thrilled and delighted. What a spectacular birthday present! It is to my great relief that Peter was in Brisbane, and not Wagga Wagga, or Brenda's telephone bills would have been sky high!

In 1984, Mum flew to Australia at the age of 85, to spend six weeks with Peter and Val in Brisbane, and she came back a different woman, knowing at last that her beloved son was still alive.

Sadly, although we didn't know it at the time, Peter was just starting to suffer with a particularly vicious version of Parkinson's Disease, and as his illness worsened Val insisted on taking him to New Zealand with her, where the finest Parkinson's doctors were practising. For 11 years until he died in July, 1994 Val was an absolute saint, and sacrificed everything to care for him and make his final years happy. It was 35 years since I last saw him when we caught up with him in 1991, and Rodney and I managed to visit him a few times before he died – it was tough seeing my once strong, handsome brother deteriorate in the cruellest way.

When Val rang me to tell me the sad news of Peter's death, I went to tell Mum. She took it with the same stoicism that had seen her through all the hard times in her life. I was able to get a flight to New Zealand, and was able to say farewell to my beloved Peter, my hero. He looked so peaceful, and I could only be happy that his suffering was over.

Joanie And Fred

When Joanie and Fred arrived back in England in 1954, they went straight to live with Fred's Mum in Shorncliffe Road, off the Old Kent Road. Fred was able to get his old job back with Otis Lifts, and in 1956 they were blessed with a son, David – a brother for Denise. I proudly became his Godmother at his Christening. Every Wednesday after school I would walk from the Bricklayer's Arms to Shorncliffe Road and spend the evening with them. Mum would join me there from work and we would watch TV – we didn't have one ourselves, so it was the only chance I got to see it. Denise and David were beautiful children and were growing up fast.

Joanie and Fred eventually bought a house in Croydon, and although they moved house a couple of times, they always remained in the general vicinity of Croydon.

As a child I had always looked up to Joanie, as she had always seemed so much older than me, but as I 'caught her up', marrying and having children, our relationship became very much closer. When I became her 'equal' we were able to have a lot of fun, and we had a lot in common. We shared the responsibility of an ageing Mum between us, taking turns to have her to stay and make sure she had all she wanted.

In 1993, Fred finally succumbed to Motor Neurone Disease, along with several other complications including cancer of the bladder, and he died in September that year. We were all devastated; he was such a lovely man.

Then, in June 1994, my darling sister Joanie died from a pulmonary embolism. This was totally unexpected and I was heartbroken. I had to break the news to Mum, and she took it calmly, her toughness and courage dictating that she dealt with it with great dignity.

Joanie had been my best friend as well as my sister, and I miss her still.

Brenda

Brenda and I corresponded regularly after I returned from Australia, and we shared by letter all the milestones, like marriage and having children, in our lives. She married Bob, a farrier, in 1961 and they eventually had two sons, Graham and Geoffrey.

Brenda and Graham visited England in 1975, and we had a great week together.

Rodney and I have been to stay with Brenda and Bob several times since our first visit in 1991, and Brenda and Bob came to England a second time to stay with us in Norwich.

In June, 2001 Brenda celebrated her 60th birthday, Bob celebrated his 65th birthday, and they were also celebrating their 40th wedding anniversary. A big party was arranged at St John's Church Hall, and I was able to turn up as a surprise guest. It was such a pleasure to be able to celebrate such a momentous occasion with them.

We now keep in touch by email, and Brenda's friendship is one of the things I really treasure. I am eternally grateful that she had the courage to befriend me at a time when I most needed a friend.

Aunty Cora

I am embarrassed to say it, but after all that Aunty Cora and her wonderful family had done for us, our correspondence lapsed. However, early in 1999 I was delighted to receive a letter from Jeanie, one of Aunty Cora's daughters. Jeanie was a few years younger than me so we hadn't really spent much time together when I was in Australia, but I remembered her from the time we spent at Aunty Cora's just before we left for England. Jeanie and her husband Jim were planning a trip to the UK, and asked if we could meet. She reminded me that she still had my old school attaché case with 'Dorothy Baker' written inside the lid, which she had inherited from me when we left Australia. I was thrilled to have them to stay for a few days, and from the moment they arrived a friendship that had started so long ago was revived, and a strong bond still exists today. When Rodney and I subsequently visited Australia, we stayed with Jeanie and Jim, and enjoyed their company so much. It also gave me the chance to renew my acquaintance with the rest of the family (including Mark, a son born in 1955 after we left Australia), but especially Aunty Cora. She hadn't changed at all, she was still the loving, kind and generous lady she had always been, and to be enveloped in her arms in a huge hug was a pleasure and a privilege.

In June, 2001 I returned to Australia on a surprise visit, which Jeanie helped me to arrange, for Aunty Cora's 90th birthday. Aunty Cora was going to celebrate her birthday with a big party at The Corowa Sports and Citizen's Club. I was so thrilled to be included in the celebrations with the whole family, and she was really pleased to see me. It was a truly memorable day, a remarkable tribute to a remarkable lady.

Sadly, at the age of 95, Aunty Cora passed away, but she will always remain special in my heart, an oasis of kindness and friendship at a time when Mum and I needed it most.

Me

Mum took me to the Education Department at the Headquarters of London County Council in County Hall. She explained that we had just returned from Australia, that I had not taken the 11-plus examination because we had left before I was due to take it, and that she had a letter from the Headmaster in Australia outlining my academic capabilities. We were asked to wait, for us it seemed like forever, and then we were shown into a gentleman's office. He asked us to sit down, then Mum explained all over again what the situation was. He was very surprised when she said that she had not opened the letter because it was addressed to 'To Whom It May Concern'. She handed the envelope over and he opened it. He read it with a grave face, and my heart sank. Then he peered over the top of his spectacles, smiled at me and said "*Well, young lady, you should be very proud of this letter!*". It transpired that Mr Bryan had written a glowing report of my achievements and my behaviour, and he stated that my IQ was 132 – not bad for a 13 year-old! The gentleman left his office for about ten minutes, during which time Mum gave me a cuddle and said how proud she was of me. When he returned, we were told that I had been placed at St. Saviour's and St Olave's Grammar School for Girls at the Bricklayer's Arms in the Old Kent Road, and that we should report there at 9.30am the next day. He gave Mum a letter of introduction to the Headmistress, Miss Collins, and then he shook our hands and wished us good luck.

The next day we duly reported at the school, and I spent the rest of my education there. At first the girls all asked me to talk, say anything, because they liked to hear the Australian accent. It gradually receded, however, and the novelty wore off as the old familiar London accent took over. Some people that I meet nowadays say that they can still detect the remnants of the Australian accent in my speech, though.

I had to work hard because by now I had slipped back to being a year behind everyone else due to the Australian education system, and I was unable to study Latin or German because I would have been three years behind in these subjects, never having started to learn them. However, I loved being at St Saviour's. I was the youngest pupil to be awarded Netball Colours for representing the school in tournaments; I gained 6 GCE's, including Maths with honours; and I made some great friends.

One of the first things we did was to go down to Seaford in Sussex to stay with Aunty Ethel and Uncle George. Flossie was looking in wonderful health, and I swear she recognised me! She wagged her tail until it was in danger of falling off, and snuggled up to me as I bent down to cuddle her. We decided that it would be unfair to take her back, as Aunty Ethel and Uncle George had grown very fond of her, but fortunately we subsequently made many visits down there so I was able to see a lot of her until she sadly died, a sedate old lady of 13 years.

There was no question of Mum being able to afford for me to stay on for Sixth Form, or go to University. I was a young adult, and had to pay my way. In 1957, at the age of 16 I left school and went to work for a stockbroker company, Phillips and Drew, in the City. I loved the work, and became the first female to speak directly to the Dealers on the floor of the Stock Exchange, which until then had been an all-male establishment.

When I was 17 I met Rodney, my husband, who was then a Metropolitan Policeman. We married when I was 19, and then moved out to Suffolk. We have three beautiful children, two daughters and a son, and we have five lovely grand-daughters.

I worked at several part-time and temporary jobs whilst the children were young, and in 1974 I went to work for Shell UK Exploration and Production Ltd at Lowestoft in Suffolk. During this time I worked hard at a part-time course at Ipswich College in order to gain Chartered Membership of the Chartered Institute of Personnel and Development, and finally retired after 14 years service having reached the position of Head of Personnel Services.

My dislike of all things Australian was very strong when I arrived back in England, and in fact it stayed with me for many years. For instance, I would not watch the Wimbledon tennis tournament on TV if Australians were playing (so I missed some wonderful Rod Laver, Margaret Court, and Yvonne Goolagong matches!); I wouldn't buy anything made in Australia; I wouldn't read any Australian books; and in general, I avoided anything connected with Australia. Also, after a few years had passed, I suffered some skin cancers on my legs, and this cemented my resentment of the time I spent there.

Rodney achieved the rank of Chief Superintendent, from which he retired in 1991. We planned to do a world trip, and one of the questions he asked me was "*Where do you want to visit in Australia?*". I was taken aback, and said "*You know how I feel about Australia, I don't want to go there*". He patiently pointed out to me that I had been harbouring a grudge for 36 years, and it was time I set it aside. The more I thought about it, the more I realised that he was right so I agreed to go. I contacted Brenda and she was only too happy to have us stay.

Our trip took us to India, Thailand, Australia, New Zealand, Fiji, Hawaii and America. We spent three months in Australia at the end of 1991, and our first port of call was Corowa. How strange it was to revisit all the places that I had known so well! The High School had been relocated to the old showground, and the showground had been relocated to South Corowa. The garage that we lived in had been pulled down, and the house and garage had been rebuilt. The house in King Street had long gone, and the land now forms part of the council yard. The houses in Whitehead Street and Betterment Parade were still there, and the hospital hadn't changed much. Sanger Street still looked the same, the War Memorial still standing proudly at the top. The beautiful old Council Offices had been replaced with a modern building, but the little shop just near them was still there. The whole visit laid so many ghosts to rest, and I was so grateful to

Rodney for insisting that I return there. Brenda and her husband Bob gave us such a wonderful holiday, and then we travelled up the east coast to Cairns, across the top and up to Darwin, and back down through the centre of Australia visiting Alice Springs, Ayers Rock, Coober Pedy and Adelaide before we flew out of Melbourne. We both love the country now, and are planning more visits back there.

On one of our visits back to Australia I was able to catch up with 'Phippa' Lethbridge, the little golden-haired boy that we babysat for, now of course a handsome grown man, and a Partner in the firm of Lethbridge and McGowan Pty. in Corowa. I was pleased to be able to give him some of the photographs that Mum had taken of him and his family back in the 1950s.

In 1993 Rodney and I returned to Australia, and Brenda organised a school reunion with some of the girls who had been at the Primary School and the High School with me. Some of them remembered the treatment that they had meted out to me, and apologised. This, more than anything else, allowed me to put all the resentment behind me, and I have been back to Australia several times since and enjoyed every minute of it.

And so ... there is a happy ending. What Australia did for me was to equip me to deal with life's challenges. And what did I do for Australia? Maybe I helped to bring a change in attitude to immigrants, maybe not – but Mum and I between us certainly gave them food for thought!

Printed in the United Kingdom by
Lightning Source UK Ltd., Milton Keynes
141815UK00001B/12/P